AFP World News Report 7

Makoto Shishido
Kevin Murphy
Mariko Takahashi

SEIBIDO

photographs by
AFP＝時事通信

DVD / Streaming Materials

LESSON 1 : © WILLIAM EDWARDS / AFPTV / DIFFERENT VIEW PHOTOGRAPHY FOR IBM & PROMARE / IBM & PROMARE / AFP

LESSON 2 : © WILLIAM EDWARDS, ARMAN SOLDIN, STUART GRAHAM / AFPTV / AFP

LESSON 3 : © ANTOINE DEMAISON, AYHAM KHALAF / AFPTV / AFP

LESSON 4 : © TINA SMOLE / AFPTV / AFP

LESSON 5 : © JÉROME PIN / AFPTV / AFP

LESSON 6 : © FAYRUZ RAJPAR / AFPTV / AFP

LESSON 7 : © SOLAN KOLLI / AFPTV / AFP

LESSON 8 : © LAMBERT NGOUANFO, STUART GRAHAM, DIANA SIMEONOVA, FRED DUFOUR / AFPTV / AFP

LESSON 9 : © SAM KINGSLEY / AFPTV / AFP

LESSON 10: © CAMILLE LAFFONT / AFPTV / AFP

LESSON 11: © SOLANGE UWIMANA, FABIEN DALLOT, AGNES COUDURIER, THEO MATTIOLO / AFPTV / QUAI BRANLY / AFPTV / POOL / AFP

LESSON 12: © JEREMIE RICHARD / AFPTV / JAKOB CECIL HAFSTEINSSON / AFP

LESSON 13: © AFPTV / TVNZ / AFP

LESSON 14: © RENAUD MASBEYE BOYBEYE / AFPTV / AFP

LESSON 15: © RAPHAEL AMBASU / AFPTV / ZION RECORD MEDIA / MONUSCO / ESN / AFP

LESSON 16: © RAPHAELLE LOGEROT / AFPTV / AFP

StreamLine

Web 動画・音声ファイルのストリーミング再生について

CD マーク及び Web 動画マークがある箇所は、PC、スマートフォン、タブレット端末において、無料でストリーミング再生することができます。下記 URL よりご利用ください。再生手順や動作環境などは本書巻末の「Web 動画のご案内」をご覧ください。

https://st.seibido.co.jp

音声ファイルのダウンロードについて

CD マークがある箇所は、ダウンロードすることも可能です。下記 URL の書籍詳細ページにあるダウンロードアイコンをクリックしてください。

https://www.seibido.co.jp/ad692

AFP World News Report 7

LINGUAPORTA

リンガポルタのご案内

> リンガポルタ連動テキストをご購入の学生さんは、
> 「リンガポルタ」を無料でご利用いただけます！

　本テキストで学習していただく内容に準拠した問題を、オンライン学習システム「リンガポルタ」で学習していただくことができます。PCだけでなく、スマートフォンやタブレットでも学習できます。単語や文法、リスニング力などをよりしっかり身に付けていただくため、ぜひ積極的に活用してください。

　リンガポルタの利用にはアカウントとアクセスコードの登録が必要です。登録方法については下記ページにアクセスしてください。

https://www.seibido.co.jp/linguaporta/register.html

本テキスト「AFP World News Report 7」のアクセスコードは下記です。

7288-2048-1231-0365-0003-0078-2E7J-N7L1

・リンガポルタの学習機能（画像はサンプルです。また、すべてのテキストに以下の4つの機能が用意されているわけではありません）

● 多肢選択

問題 2
英文を完成させるのに最も適切な語句を選びましょう。

Computers are useful, _____ they may also cause various health problems.
○ but　○ so　○ because　○ and

解答する

● 空所補充（音声を使っての聞き取り問題も可能）

問題 3
音声を聞き、空所に適切な語を入れましょう。

▶ ⏸

Experts say some workers _____ in their jobs, many have found new one _____ after reshuffling throughout the past few years. But _____ is staying put of their own volition. Some workers still _____ , but with a slowdown in uncertain economic forecast.

解答する

● 単語並びかえ（マウスや手で単語を移動）

問題 3
日本語の意味となるように、与えられた語を下線の上に並べ替え、文を完成しましょう。

私の両親は、私が一人で休暇に行くことを許可しました。
My parents _____ vacation alone.

me　on　allowed　go　to

解答する

● マッチング（マウスや手で単語を移動）

問題 3
Match the following English with its Japanese definition.

complain	（労力・時間・金など）を節約する
celebrate	（こと）を制限・限定する
restrict	満足させる
save	〜を祝う
satisfy	不平（不満・文句）を言う

解答する

はじめに

　本書は，AFP-World Academic Archive の映像ニュースで取り上げられた，世界中で起こるさまざまな最新の話題に触れながら，初中級レベルの英語力を養成することを目的としています。英語を聞き，理解する力，英文を読み，内容を理解する力，各課のテーマについて自らの意見を考え，発表をする力を養成するために必要と考える練習問題を，さまざまな工夫を凝らし配列しています。利用する学生が興味を引くような身近な社会の話題について，AFP のニュース映像と読みやすい英文を利用し，基礎的な英語理解力を高めるとともに，英語を聴く力，読む力，意見を述べる力を養成することを主眼とした，初中級者向けの教材です。

　本書の構成は下記のような特徴を持っています。

1. Listening は，AFP WAA のニュース映像を各課の話題への導入として利用しています。学生に各課のテーマについて興味を持たせる役割を持っています。

　1. Key Word Study は，ニュース映像に出てくる基礎的な重要単語を学ぶことで，話題への理解と単語力の強化を目指します。

　2. Listening Practice−First Viewing は，ニュース映像の全体像を理解するための T/F 形式の問題です。

　3. Listening Practice 2 は，細かな音の聞き取りを確認するディクテーションの問題です。

　4. Comprehension Check−Second Viewing は，さらに詳細な内容を理解しているか確認するための練習問題です。

　5. Summary は，映像で紹介されたニュースの要旨を理解しているか，最終的に確認する問題です。音声を聞き，空所を補充する形式となっています。

2. Reading は，英文読解を通じて各課のニュース映像で紹介された問題事例の内容を展開させ，さまざまな意見を紹介するものです。この英文は中心となる話題や意見の提示で，比較的容易に英語で書かれた 280 語前後の英文読解です。現代社会で話題となっている諸問題に関する情報を読むばかりでなく，基本的な英語力，単語力，読解力，思考力を身につけることを目指しています。

　1. Vocabulary Check は，英文の中で取り上げられている基礎的な英単語の学習です。

　2. Comprehension Questions は，英文の内容理解を問う問題です。学生が自ら英語で答える形式の問になっています。

　3. Grammar Check は，基本的な文法事項の確認を兼ねた語順整序演習です。

3. Discussion では，学生が積極的に参加する対話型講義への展開として，問題解決型学習（Problem Based Learning）に基づいた学生の意見を発表させることを目指しております。各課で提示される問題に関して，解決策やその理由について自らの意見をまとめ，個々の学生による発表，グループごとの発表，ディベート形式での討論など指導者の裁量でさまざまな展開が可能であると考えます。

　以上 3 部のさまざまな練習問題から，現代社会で話題となっている事柄について英語で考えながら，単語力，聴解力，読解力，文法理解力，発話力，討論力など総合的な英語能力の養成に役立つでしょう。本書を活用し，英語力の一層の向上と，社会におけるさまざまな最新情報に対する正しい理解が図られ，健全な社会生活を送るための一助となることを願います。

　最後になりましたが，本書の編集，出版にあたり，ひとかたならぬご尽力を賜った㈱成美堂，萩原美奈子氏に心より感謝申し上げます。

2023 年 9 月

著者一同

Contents

First autonomous ship prepares for maiden voyage from UK

自動運転技術が進歩しています。自律型の技術を使うことで起こりうる問題や倫理的な問題に対処しつつ,誰もがそのメリットを享受できるようにするにはどうすれば良いでしょうか。

I Listening

1 Key Word Study — Before Watching the Video —

Match each word with its definition.

1. adjustment ( ) 　 2. autonomous ( ) 　 3. avoidance ( )

4. collision ( ) 　 5. cramped ( ) 　 6. perspective ( )

7. predecessor ( ) 　 8. settler ( ) 　 9. vessel ( )

10. voyage ( )

a．先人	b．調整	c．観点	d．衝突
e．回避	f．自律型の	g．移民	h．狭苦しい
i．船舶	j．航海		

2 Listening Practice 1 — First Viewing — (Time 02:28) WEB動画 DVD

Watch the news clip and write T if the statement is true or F if it is false.

1. The *Mayflower 400* is an unmanned autonomously navigating vessel. ( )

2. Cameras on the boat see a threat and AI plots a new course to avoid a collision. ( )

3. It will be the first unmanned vessel to cross the Pacific Ocean. ( )

4. The team of engineers is aiming at commercial applications of the technology. ( )

5. It may take two weeks for the *Mayflower 400* to complete the voyage. ( )

3 Listening Practice 2   DVD CD (1-03)

Listen to the recording and fill in the missing words.

Narrator: The *Mayflower 400* is on a collision course. A small boat is in its path. But its cameras see the threat and its artificial intelligence

5   plots a new course. Collision avoided. It's a good result for software engineer Matthew Shaw who's monitoring this sea trial.

Matthew Shaw: It's very good to see. There's a lot of work and development been ¹(   ) (   )

10   (   ) (   ) (   )
    (   ) and it's nice to see it working in a real-life situation.

Narrator: The *Mayflower 400* team hope it will be the first unmanned

15   vessel to navigate across the Atlantic Ocean. Following in the wake of its namesake which took settlers from England to America 400 years ago, it will sail from Plymouth, UK to Plymouth, Massachusetts. Meirwen is helping

20   make final adjustments and says there's a lot of work still to do before the ship sails in May.

Meirwen Jenking-Rees: It's possible. It's just a bit of a struggle that we're ²(   ) (   )
    (   ) (   ) (   ), so we

25   haven't been able to go out in full choppy ocean waves, wind, rain, the full sort of worst-case-scenario stuff hasn't been achieved yet.

Narrator: As space for a crew isn't needed, the inside of the ship is

30   cramped. But there will be room for several science experiments—measuring sea levels, ³(   ) (   )
    (   ) (   ) (   )
    (   ), and recording audio to track whale

Mayflower メイフラワー号（1620年 Pilgrim Fathers を乗せて英国から新大陸の Cape Cod へ 66日かけて運んだ船）

unmanned 無人の

namesake 同名のもの

Plymouth, UK 英国プリマス（1620年メイフラワー号の出港地）
Plymouth, Massachusetts 米国マサチューセッツ州の港町プリマス（1620年メイフラワー号の到着地点）

choppy 三角波の立つ

35 populations. The hope is that autonomous ships will allow collection of much more data than manned vessels alone.

Brett Phaneuf: If we can do that—remaining safe in terms of other people on the ocean, other ships on the ocean and
40 also dealing with whatever the ocean can throw at us from a weather perspective—[if] the AI systems can do that, that's a huge move forward into reducing the cost of going to sea to collect the data that we need to understand the planet better, and that's really the
45 ultimate goal.

[if] 映像音声にはないが，文法的に付加した。

Narrator: The ship will be monitored from land using the cameras and sensors aboard and can be remotely controlled in an emergency. The

50 AI captain has been trained using thousands of images and collision avoidance rules that it gradually learns from.

Oliver Thompson: We don't have to show her every single boat she'll ever see for her to know that that particular
55 boat is a boat. There are common features, and that applies to the decisions she makes as well. So there are common features ⁴( ) ( ) ( ) ( ) ( ) that she can apply to all the scenarios she's in.

60 **Narrator:** The team say they're not looking into ⁵( ) ( ) ( ) ( ) ( ) ( ). But if the three-week voyage is a success, the *Mayflower 400* could sail into the history books, just like its historic predecessor.

Watch the news clip again and answer the following questions in English.

1. From where to where will the *Mayflower 400* sail?

_____

2. Why is the inside of the ship cramped?

_____

3. What is the hope for autonomous ships ?

_____

4. What is the ultimate goal of this autonomous vessel?

_____

5. How has the AI captain been trained to avoid collisions?

_____

5 **Summary** (1-04)

Listen to the recording and complete the summary.

The *Mayflower 400* team wants to send an [1](   ) ship across the Atlantic
Ocean. It will be monitored from land using cameras and sensors. The ship can be
controlled [2](   ) in an emergency, and the AI captain has been
[3](   ) using thousands of images and collision avoidance rules. The team
⁵ hopes that the autonomous ship will [4](   ) more data than a manned
vessel. The ship will sail in May, and the team is not interested in using the technology
for commercial [5](   ). If the voyage is successful, the *Mayflower 400* will
make history.

Ⅱ Reading (1-05)

Autonomous technology, such as drones or driverless cars, is changing all areas
of life. As its use expands, it will alter how people live, work, and connect with the
world around them.

One way it will do this is by increasing efficiency. Self-driving cars, for example,
⁵ will be used throughout the day by different travelers. As the cars are always in use,
it will free parking spaces that could be better used, for instance as parks or housing.
The cars will speak with each other, thus allowing them to drive quicker and arrive
at destinations faster. The technology will also improve accessibility. For instance,

drones will be able to deliver medical
supplies to remote locations or disaster
zones. Drones can also be used in
other ways, such as for surveying,
photography, or search and rescue missions.
Accessibility also allows more freedom
for people with disabilities, the elderly,
and those living in remote areas. For

example, robots can bring food, medicine, and other items to people who live in
areas without easy access to stores or public transport. As well as increased
efficiency and accessibility, autonomous technology will create new businesses. For
example, self-driving cars can be used for ride-sharing services, saving people
money on transport costs. Robots will be used to clean public spaces, security drones
will be used to patrol large areas, and hospitals will use medical robots to perform
surgeries.

The introduction of autonomous technology will change things in ways that, for
now, society cannot fully grasp. But as technology continues to develop, it will
reshape the ways that people interact with their surroundings and the world around
them.

(274 words)

1 Vocabulary Check

Fill in the blanks with the most appropriate word from the list below.

1. Sleep deprivation causes a drop in the (　　　　　　) of work.
2. The use of filters can (　　　　　) the appearance of photos.
3. The pilot had to change the (　　　　　) of the flight due to an emergency.
4. Japanese onomatopoeia is a difficult concept to (　　　　).
5. The team flew a drone to (　　　　　) the area for potential landslides.

| grasp | alter | survey | destination | efficiency |

2 Comprehension Questions

Answer the following questions in English.

1. How will the use of self-driving cars help people arrive at their destinations faster?

_____

2. Where can drones deliver medical supplies to improve accessibility?

_____

3. What other examples of the use of drones were mentioned?

_____

4. How are ride-sharing services beneficial for people?

_____

5. What is one use for robots in the medical field?

_____

3 Grammar Check

Unscramble the following words and complete the sentences.

1. The solution to the problem [be, to, situations, could, other, applied].

The solution to the problem [   ].

2. There is a good network [transport, in, of ,the, cities, all, public, large] in Japan.

There is a good network [   ] in Japan.

3. The study monitored the participants' [the, of, throughout, smartphones, use, day].

The study monitored the participants' [   ].

Ⅲ Discussion

インターネットなどを利用し，自動運転と事故を起こした場合の責任について調べましょう。自律型技術を使うことで起こりうる問題や倫理的な問題に対処しつつ，誰もがそのメリットを享受できるようにするにはどうすれば良いでしょうか。自動運転に伴う問題点，その責任の問題の解決方法について検討し，主張，理由など自らの考えをまとめ，発表しましょう。

自動運転の問題点について調べてみましょう。

Manufacturer	Driver/Operator
(例) hacker 　　 malfunction	(例) carelessness 　　 drunken driving

Discussion Topic

How can we deal with the problems and ethical issues that might come from using autonomous technology while making sure everyone benefits from its advantages?

Memo

Opinion

The seaweed-eating sheep helping tackle climate change

環境の変化が動植物に与えた影響について調べましょう。人間の活動や環境の変化は，動物が食べ物を探すときの適応や行動にどのような影響を与えるのでしょうか。

I Listening

1 Key Word Study — Before Watching the Video —

Match each word with its definition.

1. compound　（　）　2. disrupt　（　）　3. distinctive　（　）

4. feast on　（　）　5. flock　（　）　6. foreshore　（　）

7. inspiration　（　）　8. livestock　（　）　9. necessity　（　）

10. tide　（　）

a．独特の	b．必需品	c．磯辺	d．家畜
e．鼓舞	f．（〜というごちそうを）大いに食べる		
g．群れ	h．潮	i．妨害する	j．化合物

2 Listening Practice 1 — First Viewing — (Time 02:30) WEB動画 DVD

Watch the news clip and write T if the statement is true or F if it is false.

1. The sheep of North Ronaldsay are the only sheep that eat seaweed. （　）

2. The islanders built a dyke to keep the sheep on the seashore. （　）

3. There is plenty of grass for the sheep to eat on the island. （　）

4. The greenhouse effect of CO_2 is stronger than that of methane. （　）

5. The sheep on the island can cope with being on long grass all the time. （　）

Narrator: There's something rather unusual about the sheep of North Ronaldsay. In fact, they're unique. As the tide goes out, it's lunchtime. And they come down onto the beach to feast on seaweed. While they're not the only

5 sheep that eat the marine plants, they are thought to be the only breed for which it makes up most of their diet. That's because of the history here, where islanders built a wall, or "dyke," to keep the animals on the seashore—as sheep farmer Sinclair Scott explains.

10 **Sinclair Scott:** There was no spare grass anywhere in this island, [1](   ) (   ) (   )
(   ) (   ) (   ). They didn't have room for sheep. And gradually the sheep got pushed out and dykes got built, and they gradually

15 extended all the way around the island.

Narrator: A necessity for centuries, now the flock's diet is being used as inspiration in [2](   )
(   ) (   )

20 (   ) (   ). Scientists at the James Hutton Institute in Dundee are investigating whether a seaweed diet can reduce the amount of methane animals produce. An organic compound found in the plants is thought to disrupt methane production.

25 Sheep and cow belches might sound like a small issue— but the greenhouse effect of methane is 25 times stronger than that of carbon dioxide. And at the scale of global livestock production, that's a big problem. The scientists are adding seaweed to animal feed and

30 monitoring the results. But there's a long way to go.

Gordon McDougall: The main thing at the moment is we need to absolutely prove one, which seaweed is going to be the best for this,

North Ronaldsay ノース・ロナルドセー島（スコットランド，オークニー諸島北端の島）
seaweed 海藻

dyke 堤防

James Hutton Institute
ジェームズハットン研究所

methane メタン

belch げっぷ

35   [3](   ) (   ) (   )
(   ) into the feed gives the best effect. And then, can you scale that up to a level where you'd actually have an effect on the overall UK farming?

Narrator: Back in the north of the Orkney Isles, the industries
40   which brought hundreds of people here in the 18th and 19th centuries [4](   ) (   ) (   ) (   ). Keeping the dykes in good repair is getting more difficult—but it's still just as important for the welfare of the sheep, because they've
45   become so well adapted to the seaweed.

Sinclair Scott: After the sheep had been excluded for many years, then they found that they couldn't cope with being on grass, long
50   grass, all the time. So sheep that have gone from here to England and places like that have a habit of dying.

Narrator: Keeping the sheep on the foreshore is important for another reason too—their seaweed diet
55   gives their meat a distinctive flavor, making it much sought after—it's even been served to the Queen. So [5](   ) (   ) (   ) (   ) (   ) (   ) (   ) (   ) it's
60   hoped that North Ronaldsay's traditions can continue for generations to come.

4 Comprehension Check — Second Viewing —

Watch the news clip again and answer the following questions in English.

1. What is unique about the sheep of North Ronaldsay?

   _____

2. How did the sheep start to live on the foreshore?

   _____

3. What is the James Hutton Institute investigating?

   _____

4. Why is keeping the dykes in good condition important?

   _____

5. Why is keeping the sheep on the foreshore important?

   _____

5 Summary

 CD(1-08)

Listen to the recording and complete the summary.

While they are not the only sheep that eat seaweed, the sheep of North Ronaldsay
are thought to be the only [1](   ) for which it makes up most of their diet.
Scientists at the James Hutton Institute in Dundee are investigating whether a
seaweed diet can [2](   ) the amount of methane animals produce. Keeping
5   the dykes in good [3](   ) is getting more difficult, but it's still important for
the welfare of the sheep, because they have become so well adapted to the seaweed.
After the sheep had been [4](   ) for many years, it was found that they
couldn't cope with being on grass all the time. Keeping the sheep on the foreshore is
important for another reason too. Their seaweed diet gives their meat a distinctive
10   [5](   ), making it much sought after. It has even been served to the Queen.

II Reading

 CD(1-09)

Human activity has forced many animals to adapt to new environments, more
specifically, the food choices available to them and how they evolve to ingest it. The
natural habitats of many species have faced significant changes due to growing
urban areas, farming, and deforestation. To cope with these broad changes, wildlife
5   must alter their feeding habits, activities, and, in some cases, their physical structure.

      Many city birds have learned to locate and use packaged foods, changing how they act in response to increased amounts of human trash. Studies show that human food waste can have fewer nutrients and harms their immune systems. In the same way, common wild animals such as foxes and raccoons have adapted to urban settings by changing their behavior in new ways. They have

learned to feed in gardens, avoid traffic, and dig in trash cans. The shift from their usual diet impacts their health and increases the numbers of their natural prey, such as rabbits and mice. The fishing industry has also shared the impact of human-led change. Overfishing has caused fish stocks to adapt, increasing the number of smaller fish. Fish that mature at smaller sizes are less likely to be caught by predators and more likely to breed. Moreover, many insects and other pests have evolved to resist farm pesticides, altering their diet and life cycle. They now safely consume many of the chemicals, highlighting the marked impact of human actions on animal evolution.

Humans have forced many animal species to adapt their behavior in pursuit of food. These adaptations significantly affect many forms of life, including humans, over time and continue to effect change in the ecosystems in which they survive.

(280words)

1 Vocabulary Check

Fill in the blanks with the most appropriate word from the list below.

1. The main (   ) of koalas is the eucalypt forests of Australia.
2. Household cats learn to meow in (   ) to their owner's calls.
3. Kiwis lost their ability to fly because there were no (   ) that threatened them.
4. Pandas (   ) up to 38 kilograms of bamboo every day.
5. The researchers were able to (   ) the lion pride they were looking for.

habitat	consume	predators	locate	response

2 Comprehension Questions

Answer the following questions in English.

1. Why have the natural habitats of animals faced significant changes?

2. What are the demerits of human food waste for city birds?

3. What have wild animals such as foxes and raccoons learned to do?

4. What is an outcome of overfishing?

5. How have insects and pests evolved to resist farm pesticides?

3 Grammar Check

Unscramble the following words and complete the sentences.

1. Seaweed helps to sustain marine life, [an, releasing, amount, adequate, oxygen, of] into water.

   Seaweed helps to sustain marine life, [   ] water.

2. In Australia, many unique [country, animals, species, evolved, the, as, of] was separated from the rest of the world more than 30 million years ago.

   In Australia, many unique [   ] was separated from the rest of the world more than 30 million years ago.

3. The city government implemented [to, measures, number, with, increasing, new, the, cope] of wild cats in the area.

   The city government implemented [   ] of wild cats in the area.

III Discussion

インターネットなどを利用し，環境の変化が動植物に与えた影響について調べましょう。人間の活動や環境の変化は，動物が食べ物を探すときの適応や行動にどのような影響を与えるのでしょうか。動物が新しい環境に適応する際の問題点，その問題の解決方法について検討し，主張，理由など自らの考えをまとめ，発表しましょう。

新しい環境に適応した生物について，どのような影響を与えているのか調べてみましょう。

Animals/Plants	Consequences
(例)crows in urban areas	(例)noisy

Discussion Topic

How does human activity and environmental change influence the way animals adapt and behave when it comes to finding food?

Memo

Opinion

Video game developers cash in on Africa's booming market

ビジネスのグローバル化，ローカル化について考えましょう。自治体や地域の人々が協力して，企業の成長を助け，企業と地域のつながりをより強くするためには，どうしたら良いでしょうか。

I Listening

1 Key Word Study ─ Before Watching the Video ─

Match each word with its definition.

1. deconstruct (   )   2. immense   (   )   3. infrastructure (   )

4. massive   (   )   5. pave   (   )   6. revolutionary   (   )

7. sector   (   )   8. specific   (   )   9. spike   (   )

10. tap   (   )

a．基盤設備	b．大規模な	c．道を開く	d．特定の
e．革命的な	f．分野	g．増加	h．計り知れない
i．～を解体する	j．開発する		

2 Listening Practice 1 ─ First Viewing ─

(Time 02:57)   WEB動画 📖📱 💿DVD

Watch the news clip and write T if the statement is true or F if it is false.

1. Gamers in Africa have more than tripled in recent years.   (   )

2. Each of the African languages is linked to a specific culture that has different histories.   (   )

3. Africa's largest gathering for gaming was held in Cape Town earlier this year.   (   )

4. Kossoko has been creating games that tell stories of the world since 2018. (   )

5. Kossoko hopes his games can eventually compete against those developed by large companies.   (   )

3 Listening Practice 2

Listen to the recording and fill in the missing words.

Narrator: It is just the beginning for video gaming in Africa. Gamers have more than doubled in recent years. The market's untapped

5   potential is immense, with many expecting it to explode as the continent produces more content. Until recently, gamers mostly came from the United States, Europe, and Japan. But a shift is underway. There is a big market waiting to be tapped, according to South African

10   developer Alexander Poone.

Alexander Poone: We, for example, in South Africa have 11 different languages. That's one thing. Each of them are linked to a specific

[are] 文法的には is が正しいが，話者の音声を優先

15   culture that has different histories. Playing with that in game development as a means to telling a story, it allows you to actually [1](   ) (   ) (   ) (   ) (   ) (   ) that is new and not been fully explored

20   yet.

Narrator: Developers met at Africa's largest gathering for gaming in Cape Town earlier this year.

Nick Hall: We've got a lot of those publishers who are coming here, and they want African-made content and so

25   [2](   ) (   ) (   ) (   ). Now is kind of the best time really to be making games or trying to get into the games industry because we're hoping in the next few years, we're going to see a massive spike in growth.

30 **Narrator:** Poor infrastructure and low connectivity have held back gaming on the continent. But Internet speeds and access are improving, [3](   ) (   ) (   ). Central African Teddy Kossoko is paving the way for the new market. Since 2018, he has

connectivity 接続性

35　been creating games that tell the story of Africa.

Teddy Kossoko: For me, the future of  this industry, and not only this industry, is in Africa. It's the new El Dorado. Centuries ago, there

40　was a gold rush in America. Today, I believe this gold rush is happening here on the African continent, and we have to be first.

Narrator: Kossoko moved to France aged  18 to study computer science and

45　management. He started a studio in　Toulouse　[4](　　　　　) (　　　　　) (　　　　　) (　　　　　　　). One of the Masseka Game Studio's creations allows players to use avatars of African heroes—like Burkina Faso's

50　revolutionary leader Thomas Sankara, South African singer Miriam Makeba, and George Weah, footballer and former president of Liberia.

Teddy Kossoko: We must teach young people to love themselves, to value themselves. There is a huge

55　problem with that. And for us, all this is at the heart of our creations. We really want people to deconstruct everything　[5](　　　　　) (　　　　　) (　　　　　) (　　　　　) (　　　　　) (　　　　　　): that they are not

60　beautiful, that they are useless.

Narrator: Creators like Kossoko hope their games can eventually compete against those developed by the heavyweights of the sector.

El Dorado 黄金郷

Thomas Sankara オートボルタ共和国（現ブルキナファソ）の第5代大統領
Miriam Makeba 南アフリカ共和国の歌手でグラミー賞受賞者
George Weah リベリア共和国出身の政治家，元サッカー選手

Comprehension Check — Second Viewing —

Watch the news clip again and answer the following questions in English.

1. Where did gamers mostly come from until recently?

_____

2. How many languages does South Africa have?

_____

3. What are the reasons that have prevented gaming from spreading in the African market?

_____

4. Where did Kossoko study computer science and management?

_____

5. What does one of the Masseka Game Studio's creations allow players to use?

_____

Summary

Listen to the recording and complete the summary.

Developers gathered at Africa's biggest gaming [1](   ) in Cape Town earlier this year. This is an excellent time to start creating games or break into the gaming industry, as a [2](   ) growth spike is anticipated in the next few years. Teddy Kossoko, from Central Africa, is paving the way for this new market.
5 He has been producing games that [3](   ) the story of Africa since 2018. One of Masseka Game Studio's creations allows players to use [4](   ) of African heroes. Creators like Kossoko aspire to [5](   ) with the big names in the gaming sector with their games in the future.

II Reading

Businesses are vital for helping local economies grow and develop. They give people jobs, sell products, and pay taxes. When local businesses do well, the economy and community become stronger and can deal with changes more easily.

One way that businesses help the local economy is by creating work. When
5 people have jobs, they spend more money in the local area. Spending helps the economy grow even more and supports other local businesses. Local businesses also help the economy by paying taxes. These taxes are used for community projects,

improving roads and buildings, and providing vital public services. Investment

10 is another way local businesses help the local economy. Successful businesses often put money back into the community, which allows the economy to grow. For example, they might open new stores,

15 make existing businesses bigger, invest

in new technology, or support projects in the local economy. Local economies can help small businesses grow by providing help, support, and an environment to succeed. This support encourages new ideas and better ways of doing things, which helps economic growth. Local businesses also strengthen the area by joining in local

20 events and getting to know the people there. By doing this, they can foster a sense of belonging and unity. Furthermore, local businesses can often be more environmentally friendly and buy products locally. In this way, they reduce pollution and help the environment.

Local businesses are vital in helping local economies grow. They create jobs,

25 pay taxes, keep money in the community, and invest in local projects. Making it easy for local businesses to succeed aids growth, creates a stronger sense of community, and can help protect the environment.

(275words)

Vocabulary Check

Fill in the blanks with the most appropriate word from the list below.

1. The two companies were able to hold a (   ) meeting.
2. The organization (   ) those who are in need of medical treatment.
3. It is important to look at (   ) literature before starting a new research project.
4. The workshop will (   ) a better understanding of the economic situation of the region.
5. The university (   ) students to take part in international programs.

aids	foster	existing	successful	encourages

2 Comprehension Questions

Answer the following questions in English.

1. How is spending money in the local area beneficial for the local economy?

_____

2. What are taxes paid by local businesses used for?

_____

3. What do successful businesses often do?

_____

4. How can local economies help small businesses grow?

_____

5. How do local businesses strengthen the area?

_____

3 Grammar Check

Unscramble the following words and complete the sentences.

1. The city [open, offers, to, for, businesses, grants] new stores in the area.

The city [_____] new stores in the area.

2. Ice cream produced [very, local, well, a, by, sold, dairy] at the farmers' market.

Ice cream produced [_____] the farmers' market.

3. Ethan goes to [time, he, the, when, has, library] between his classes.

Ethan goes to [_____] between his classes.

III Discussion

インターネットなどを利用し，ビジネスのグローバル化，ローカル化について調べましょう。自治体や地域の人々が協力して，企業の成長を助け，企業と地域のつながりをより強くするためには，どうしたら良いでしょうか。それぞれのビジネスの問題点，その問題の解決方法について検討し，主張，理由など自らの考えをまとめ，発表しましょう。

ビジネスのグローバル化，ローカル化
それぞれの問題点について調べてみましょう。

Globalization	Localization
(例) low cost	(例) preserving local culture

Discussion Topic

How can local governments and people in the community work together to help businesses grow and create a stronger connection between businesses and the community?

Memo

Opinion

_____

_____

_____

_____

Ugandan children back to school after nearly 2-year COVID closure

政府，学校，地域社会が協力して教育格差を解消し，裕福な生徒と貧しい生徒の双方にオンライン学習への平等なアクセスを促進するにはどうしたら良いでしょうか。

I Listening

1 Key Word Study — Before Watching the Video —
Match each word with its definition.

1. abandon　（　　）　2. authority　（　　）　3. deputy headmaster （　　）

4. dramatically （　　）　5. intervention （　　）　6. primary school　（　　）

7. privileged　（　　）　8. profession　（　　）　9. pupil　　　（　　）

10. restriction　（　　）

a．生徒	b．小学校	c．介入	d．劇的に
e．恵まれた	f．副校長	g．制限	h．当局
i．職業	j．放棄する		

2 Listening Practice 1 — First Viewing —
(Time 01:48) WEB動画 DVD

Watch the news clip and write T if the statement is true or F if it is false.

1. Students in Uganda wore their school uniforms for the first time in three years.

（　　）

2. The 15 million Ugandan students feel relieved to return to the classroom. （　　）

3. Remote learning was available for all the students in Uganda.　　　　　（　　）

4. Schools have struggled to restart since not all teachers are back.　　　（　　）

5. Some teachers in private schools did not receive any pay during the pandemic.

（　　）

Narrator: Pupils put on their uniforms again for the first day back at school. It is a special day for these Ugandans, who have had

5   scant education for 83 weeks. Ugandan schools remained closed since the COVID-19 pandemic broke out in March 2020. Returning to the classroom is [1]( ) ( ) ( ) ( ) ( ) for the 15 million

10   school children across the country, but also for their parents.

Siraj Senkungu: We have taken two years without coming to school, but now I'm very happy to see

15   the children back, and to get their friends. [2]( ) ( ) ( ) ( ) ( ).

Narrator: No other country closed schools for as long as Uganda. Remote learning was available only for the

20   most privileged.

Nawilah Senkungu: I am happy, because [3]( ) ( ) ( ) ( ) ( ) ( ) ( ) ( ) ( ).

25 **Narrator:** But not all teachers are back. Schools have struggled to restart, this primary school deputy headmaster explains.

Richard Aburo: There are teachers in private schools that did not receive any pay completely and others might

30   have even abandoned the profession, so now bridging up that gap. Still [4]( ) ( ) ( ) ( ) ( ) and we will need some serious intervention by the government.

scant 不十分な

pandemic パンデミック (全世界に広がるような，広域でまん延する深刻な感染病の大流行)

31

35 **Narrator:** Authorities vowed to keep a close eye on private schools to prevent exorbitant fees. For many Ugandans, it is even harder than [5](   ) (   ) (   ) (   ) to afford education. Various coronavirus restrictions dramatically cut into 40 incomes.

exorbitant 法外な	
coronavirus コロナウイルス	

4 Comprehension Check — Second Viewing —

Watch the news clip again and answer the following questions in English.

1. For how long did Ugandan students not attend schools because of the COVID-19 pandemic?

_____

2. Who could receive remote learning in Uganda during the pandemic?

_____

3. What happened to some private school teachers because of the pandemic?

_____

4. What did the authorities do with regard to private schools?

_____

5. How did people's incomes change during the pandemic?

_____

5 Summary CD(1-16)

Listen to the recording and complete the summary.

Schools in Uganda have been closed since March 2020 due to the COVID-19 [1](   ). The return to in-person classes is not only a great [2](   ) for the 15 million schoolchildren in the country but also for their parents. After two years of being away from school, parents are happy to see their children returning 5 to school and [3](   ) with their friends. However, restarting schools has been a struggle, especially for private schools. Some private school teachers have not received any pay, and some may have even left the profession, creating a [4](   ) gap. While it will take time to recover from these challenges, the government will need to intervene seriously. The authorities have promised to 10 [5](   ) private schools to prevent them from charging exorbitant fees.

The COVID-19 pandemic disrupted education globally, causing school closures and a shift to online learning. However, wealthier students have gained more educational benefits than their poorer peers.

One reason is the digital divide or unequal access to technology and the Internet. Poorer students often need help to afford laptops or high-speed Internet connections. It is harder for them to join online classes or access resources. In contrast, richer students can easily buy the technology that allows them to continue their education. Another factor is the learning environment. Poorer students often live in overcrowded, noisy homes, making it challenging to focus and learn. For example, they may share a computer with family members or need to study in a small space. In contrast, wealthier students may enjoy a quiet, spacious home, their own room, and a more favorable study setting. Financial stability also matters. For example, poorer students may need to work part-time, resulting in missed classes or less study time. Richer students, on the other hand, can focus on their online courses without needing to support themselves. Additionally, the need for in-person learning has highlighted contrasts in education quality. Sometimes, students with less money attend schools without the funds to provide the proper online learning support. As a result, they miss key face-to-face interactions with teachers and peers, which can hold back their education and development.

The COVID-19 crisis has widened the education gap between richer and poorer students. Factors like the digital divide, learning environment, and lack of finance have led to unequal outcomes among students. Ensuring equal access to education for all, regardless of their background, is vital for governments.

(279 words)

1 Vocabulary Check

Fill in the blanks with the most appropriate word from the list below.

1. It is (   ) for children to receive education.
2. The main building of the university has (   ) lecture halls, accommodating up to 300 students each.
3. The report (   ) both the merits and demerits of online education.

4. It is important to use (   ) grammar when writing an academic paper.

5. The university (   ) that all the students had access to digital devices to attend online classes.

| vital | ensures | proper | spacious | highlights |

2 Comprehension Questions
Answer the following questions in English.

1. How did the pandemic affect education globally?

_____

2. What is the first factor mentioned as the cause of the widening education gap?

_____

3. What is the second factor?

_____

4. How does a lack of financial stability affect educational opportunities for poorer students?

_____

5. What should governments do to help with the education gap?

_____

3 Grammar Check
Unscramble the following words and complete sentences.

1. The teacher made sure that [than, was, first, the, easier, question] the second question.

The teacher made sure that [   ] the second question.

2. Not [computers, devices, everyone, like, afford, can, digital] and smartphones.

Not [   ] and smartphones.

3. The new SNS [popular, than, out, to, turned, less, be] the existing services because it failed to introduce new features.

The new SNS [   ] the existing services because it failed to introduce new features.

Ⅲ Discussion

インターネットなどを利用し，オンライン学習への平等なアクセスについて調べましょう。政府，学校，地域社会が協力して教育格差を解消し，裕福な生徒と貧しい生徒の双方に，オンライン学習への平等なアクセスを促進するにはどうしたら良いでしょうか。オンライン学習の問題点，その問題の解決方法について検討し，主張，理由など自らの考えをまとめ，発表しましょう。

オンライン学習へのアクセスとその問題点について調べてみましょう。

Device necessary for online class	Problems
(例)PC 　　tablet 　　smart phone	(例)cost to buy equipment 　　parents are not familiar with technology

Discussion Topic

How can governments, schools, and communities work together to bridge the education gap and promote equal access to online learning for both wealthier and poorer students?

Memo

Opinion

Street art transforms Quinta do Mocho District in Lisbon

落書きか，ストリートアートか。街の中の芸術を通じて人々が自分自身を表現できるようにしながら，公共空間や私的空間を清潔で安全に保つにはどうしたら良いでしょうか。

Ⅰ Listening

1 Key Word Study — Before Watching the Video —

Match each word with its definition.

1. awaken	( )	2. boast	( )	3. curiosity	( )
4. discrimination	( )	5. inhabitant	( )	6. invisible	( )
7. plague	( )	8. resurrection	( )	9. territory	( )
10. transform	( )				

a．差別	b．～を悩ます	c．好奇心	d．～を変える
e．住民	f．領域	g．～を呼び起こす	h．復興
i．目に見えない	j．～を誇る		

2 Listening Practice 1 — First Viewing —

(Time 02:06) WEB動画 DVD

Watch the news clip and write T if the statement is true or F if it is false.

1. The Quinta do Mocho District in Lisbon was always the city's safest suburb.

( )

2. The town hall organized the first street art festival in 2014. ( )

3. There are now more than 120 paintings on the walls in the district. ( )

4. The murals have created problems such as racial discrimination. ( )

5. The street art has contributed to the increase in tourists in the area. ( )

Narrator: Quinta do Mocho District in Lisbon used to be considered one of the city's most dangerous suburbs, plagued by violence and

Quinta do Mocho District
キンタ・ド・モーショ地区

5 drugs, where even taxis refused to go. But street art has transformed the housing project and the lives of its 2,800 inhabitants, with guided visits now organized in the former ghetto.

ghetto スラム街

Emanuela Kalemba: These works of art in our neighborhood

10 have allowed us to project ourselves into the world. People come here, they want to know us, to hear our stories,

¹( ) ( ) ( )

( ). Before we were

like invisible territory, nobody

15 saw us, nobody was interested in us. Today all that has changed.

Narrator: In 2014, the town hall organized the district's first street art festival and offered to paint some of the buildings' walls. Since then, ²( )

20 ( ) ( ) ( )

( ) every year and the district now boasts more than 120 murals. About one hundred Portuguese and international artists have taken part in turning this neighborhood into an open-air street art gallery.

mural 壁画

25 **Ana Correia:** I think it's very important, both for those who come and for those who live here. It's good that there is ³( )

( ) ( ) ( ) that

30 things can be different and that all of us can contribute to creating a different atmosphere.

Narrator: The murals have also raised awareness on topics like racial discrimination, children's rights, multiculturalism, and justice.

multiculturalism 多文化主義

37

35 **Francisco Caba Silla:** These paintings on the walls
⁴(   ) (   ) (   )
(   ) (   ) (   ) , it
awakens their curiosity, creates dialogue, they try to
understand the meanings that these paintings represent
40   for our neighborhood.

Narrator: Aside from giving Quinta
do Mocho a new look, the street
art has also contributed to its
resurrection by attracting tourists.

45 **Jorge Quintas:** It's better because for a long time everything
here was abandoned, but today ⁵(   )
(   ) (   ) (   )
(   ) (   ).

Narrator: Quinta do Mocho's town hall says the initiative has
50   resulted in the opening of a bus line, the creation of
more cultural events, and a reduction in crime rates.

4 Comprehension Check — Second Viewing —

Watch the news clip again and answer the following questions in English.

1. What problems did Quinta do Mocho suffer from?

2. How many residents are living in Quinta do Mocho District?

3. How many Portuguese and international artists have taken part in the open-air street art gallery?

4. What do the paintings on the walls make children do?

5. What results does the initiative in street art bring to the district?

5 Summary

Listen to the recording and complete the summary.

Quinta do Mocho District in Lisbon used to be a dangerous suburb plagued by
[1]( ) and drugs, where taxis even refused to go. However, the town hall
[2]( ) a street art festival in 2014, and the paintings have transformed the
housing project and the lives of its 2,800 inhabitants. The district has become an
5 open-air street art [3]( ) with guided visits, which has created
[4]( ) and curiosity among the residents and their children. The street art
has also contributed to the district's resurrection by [5]( ) tourists, aside
from giving it a new look.

II Reading

Graffiti, some that dates back tens of thousands of years, is often seen in public
locations worldwide. Some people strongly believe it is a form of art that conveys
powerful messages and creativity. In contrast, others view drawing and painting in
public spaces as vandalism.

5 Many cities see graffiti as a crime because it is created outside a gallery and
marks public or private spaces without permission. Some argue this is theft, as the
artist takes control of another person's property without consent. Artists who create
graffiti can face fines or, in some cases, risk prison.

However, others argue that graffiti is a form of art and deserves protection
10 under the law. They believe graffiti is a means of communication, particularly for
underrepresented communities. Artists can use their work to make powerful
statements about social and political issues. Banksy, for example, is well-known for
creating graffiti covering various social and cultural topics. In this way, graffiti can
be a voice and a source of identity for those who feel ignored by society.

15 Graffiti has recently been recognized as a valid art form with specific areas put
aside for artists to paint. These spaces have allowed graffiti to develop and have
helped build an active street art culture. The death of George Floyd in the United
States in 2020, for example, resulted in murals painted on spaces across the world.

With valid arguments on both sides, it is difficult to decide whether graffiti is, in
20 fact, a crime or a form of art. In the end, the answer to this question will depend on
whether a viewer sees it as damage to property or a valid form of self-expression.

(281words)

❶ Vocabulary Check

Fill in the blanks with the most appropriate word from the list below.

1. The map shows the (　　　　) of the main entrance of the art museum.
2. The police secured the (　　　　) scene of a burglary.
3. The artist (　　　　) more recognition for his use of recycled materials.
4. Max often (　　　　) his mother's advice and gets into trouble.
5. This government (　　　　) cannot be used for recreational purposes.

| property location deserves crime ignores |

❷ Comprehension Questions

Answer the following questions in English.

1. Why do many cities see graffiti as a crime?

_____

2. What can happen to artists who create graffiti?

_____

3. What do people who argue graffiti deserves protection believe?

_____

4. What is Banksy well-known for?

_____

5. Why is it difficult to decide whether graffiti is a crime or a form of art?

_____

❸ Grammar Check

Unscramble the following words and complete the sentences.

1. According to the brochure, [at, sculptures, museum, displayed, of, some, the, the] date back to 5,000 years ago.

   According to the brochure, [_____]

   date back to 5,000 years ago.

2. Cindy tried to [success, vase, the, broken, without, repair, any].

   Cindy tried to [_____].

3. This [who, is, restaurant, for, recommended, those] want to try authentic local food.

   This [_____] want to try authentic local

   food.

Ⅲ Discussion

インターネットなどを利用し，ストリートアートや落書きについて調べましょう。ストリートアートを通じて人々が自分自身を表現できるようにしながら，公共空間や私的空間を清潔で安全に保つにはどうしたら良いでしょうか。ストリートアートや落書きの問題点，その問題の解決方法について検討し，主張，理由など自らの考えをまとめ，発表しましょう。

ストリートアートと落書きの違いや，その問題点について調べてみましょう。

Street Art	Graffiti	Problems
(例) Banksy	(例) Subway in NY	(例) spoil the landscape

Discussion Topic

How can we let people express themselves through graffiti while also keeping public and private spaces clean and safe?

Memo

Opinion

Lesson 6

Waste not, want not: UK consumers use apps to fight food waste

世界的な食品廃棄の問題を解決するためにモバイルアプリを使用する場合，どのような問題や困難が考えられるでしょうか。また，これらのアプリが本当にうまく機能するには，どのようにすれば良いでしょうか。

Ⅰ Listening

1 Key Word Study — Before Watching the Video —

Match each word with its definition.

1. aviation   (   )   2. bin   (   )   3. cohesion   (   )

4. comparative (   )   5. core   (   )   6. edible   (   )

7. retailer   (   )   8. rubbish   (   )   9. surplus   (   )

10. sustainability (   )

a．航空	b．ゴミ入れ	c．ゴミ	d．余った
e．結束	f．持続可能性	g．かなりの	h．食べられる
i．本質的な	j．小売業者		

2 Listening Practice 1 — First Viewing —

(Time 02:31) WEB動画 📺 DVD

Watch the news clip and write T if the statement is true or F if it is false.

1. Jack can order his lunch with a couple of clicks on his phone.   (   )

2. The app Karma is used to sell leftover meals by 2,000 UK supermarkets. (   )

3. Seventy percent of food waste comes from restaurants in the UK.   (   )

4. The food sharing apps can solve the core problem of food waste.   (   )

5. Ten million meals a year end up in rubbish bins in the UK.   (   )

Narrator: In just a couple of clicks, Jack has ordered his lunch. But he's also helped to rescue food that would otherwise end up in the

5　rubbish bin. Jack is buying through an app called Karma, which connects users with restaurants and cafés selling their surplus food at discount prices.

Jack Convery: Anything I can do to help the environment and also [1](　　　) (　　　) (　　　)

10　(　　　) as well is beneficial, so yeah it's a win-win.

Narrator: Around 2,000 UK outlets are selling their leftover meals through the Swedish start-up. The app

15　allows participating businesses to make some money on food that [2](　　　) (　　　) (　　　) (　　　) (　　　). According to resource efficiency charity WRAP, food waste costs the British restaurant

20　sector £682 million each year. So why not just make less?

Sara McCraight: So, we don't plan for the day to end up with zero waste, because at the end of every day we do want to have some stock on our shelves, otherwise a customer

25　could walk in and see an empty store.

Narrator: But 70 percent of food waste comes from the home—with the average British family throwing out 800 pounds worth of edible produce every year. Another app, Olio, helps [3](　　　)

30　(　　　) (　　　) (　　　) (　　　) with people in their area. Its founder wants to educate users on the comparative environmental impact of food waste.

Karma スウェーデンのスタートアップが起業したスマートショッピングアプリ

win-win 一挙両得

leftover 食べ残し

WRAP (The Waste and Resources Action Programme) 廃棄物と資源に関する行動計画

Olio 英国のフリーシェアリングアプリ

43

Tessa Clarke: Roughly 10 percent of all of our annual greenhouse gas emissions come from food waste alone, which I like to point out to people is four to five times greater than the carbon emissions that come from the global aviation industry.

Narrator: But while these apps seem like a win-win for their users and for food retailers, experts say they don't solve the core problem.

Martin Caraher: These are good for raising awareness but they're not in themselves solutions, because there's still food surplus or ⁴( ) ( ) ( ) ( ). They do bring about a greater awareness, they do bring about more community. There is some evidence about community cohesion, that this is good, particularly things like Olio, that communities begin to build up around these and that's good, and then begin to look at other alternatives.

Narrator: In 2007 the UK ramped up the fight against food waste, and by 2018 had cut levels by just under 20 percent, thanks to clearer labelling and better food recycling. But according to the food sustainability index, in 2018 the UK still ranked in the top 10 high income countries ⁵( ) ( ) ( ) ( ) ( ) ( ) ( ). And with 10 billion meals a year still ending up in the bin, the UK has yet to fully close the door on the food waste problem.

4 Comprehension Check — Second Viewing —

Watch the news clip again and answer the following questions in English.

1. What is the Karma app useful for?

_____

2. How much does food waste cost the British restaurant sector each year?

_____

3. Where does 10 percent of annual greenhouse gas emissions come from?

_____

4. In pounds, how much edible produce does the average British family throw out each year?

_____

5. How did the UK cut food waste levels to under 20 percent by 2018?

_____

5 Summary (1-24)

Listen to the recording and complete the summary.

Food waste costs British restaurants £682 million annually, according to the charity WRAP. Its founder wants to educate people about the environmental ¹(   )of food waste. Although awareness-raising efforts are helpful, they are not enough on their own because food ²(   ) and waste still exist. The
5 UK made progress against food waste from 2007 to 2018 by using clearer ³(   ) and better food recycling, cutting waste by nearly 20 percent. However, in 2018, the UK still ⁴(   ) among the top 10 high-income countries with the highest levels of food loss, according to the food sustainability index. Unfortunately, 10 billion meals each year still end up in the bin, indicating
10 that the UK still has work to do to ⁵(   ) the food waste problem.

II Reading
(1-25)

Food waste is a major global problem. Up to half of all the food produced worldwide is never eaten. The result is wasted resources, money, and large amounts of food going to harmful methane-producing landfills. However, mobile telephone and tablet apps show how technology can assist with the issue. Apps are now helping
5 to reduce food waste and, as a result, are protecting the environment.

45

Mobile apps designed to tackle food waste link people with local businesses, such as supermarkets and restaurants. These places have leftover food that is regularly discarded. Customers can buy the food at lower prices, thus helping to reduce the businesses' food waste. For example, apps like Too Good To Go allow users to see a list of businesses and their available food. Users can then place an order and collect the food when it is convenient. These apps provide a way to reduce waste and a way for people to buy healthy, fresh food that might otherwise be thrown away.

Another way apps can help with the food waste problem is by providing tools that consumers can use to manage their food better at home. For example, apps such as Fridge Pal allow users to input the items they have at home and receive reminders for using the food before it goes bad. This helps reduce the amount of food that goes out of date or is forgotten.

Mobile apps can play a helpful role in reducing food waste by allowing consumers to find surplus food, giving them the tools to manage food at home, and teaching them about the issue. As technology improves and more people learn about food waste, it seems likely that more innovative apps will help tackle this global problem.

(290 Words)

1 Vocabulary Check

Fill in the blanks with the most appropriate word from the list below.

1. Cory called the restaurant to ask if there was a table (   ) for four next Tuesday.
2. Skipping breakfast is not a good way to (   ) your daily calorie intake.
3. It took me a while to figure out how to (   ) the new smartwatch to my smartphone.
4. Luke decided to purchase an annual pass for the theme park because he (   ) goes there.
5. Some companies have been developing alternative meat as an (   ) way to solve the world's food shortage.

reduce	regularly	link	innovative	available

2 Comprehension Questions

Answer the following questions in English.

1. How much food goes uneaten in the world?

_____

2. What do mobile apps that help address food waste do?

_____

3. How do customers use apps like Too Good To Go?

_____

4. How can mobile apps help consumers manage their food at home?

_____

5. Why is receiving reminders of the food at home helpful in reducing food waste?

_____

3 Grammar Check

Unscramble the following words and complete the sentences.

1. Peter decided to go to [meal, expired, ticket, restaurant, the, before, the].
   Peter decided to go to [_____].

2. You [fruits, as, enjoy, such, tropical, mango, can] and passion fruit in Hawaii.
   You [_____] and passion fruit in Hawaii.

3. One way to order pizza is by phone, [app, another, is, and, by, way].
   One way to order pizza is by phone, [_____].

III Discussion

インターネットなどを利用し，食品廃棄について調べましょう。世界的な食品廃棄の問題を解決するためにモバイルアプリを使用する場合，どのような問題や困難が考えられますか？　これらのアプリが本当にうまく機能するようにするには，どのようにこれらの問題を解決すれば良いでしょうか？　食品廃棄の問題点，その問題の解決方法について検討し，主張，理由など自らの考えをまとめ，発表しましょう。

**食品廃棄が起こりうる
場所と理由を調べてみましょう。**

Food waste	Problems
(例)supermarket 　　convenience store	(例)throw away food before they expire

Discussion Topic

What might be some problems or difficulties with using mobile apps to help solve the worldwide food waste issue?

How can we fix these problems to make sure these apps really work well?

Memo

Opinion

Ethiopian girls take on gender stereotypes at the skatepark

ジェンダー・ステレオタイプは他人を傷つけ，不公平を生む可能性があるにもかかわらず，いまだに信じている人が多いのはなぜでしょうか。このような固定概念をやめさせ，誰もが平等に扱われるようにするためにはどうしたら良いでしょうか。

I Listening

1 Key Word Study — Before Watching the Video —

Match each word with its definition.

1. civil   (   )   2. defeat   (   )   3. extreme   (   )

4. frustration   (   )   5. gendered   (   )   6. nail   (   )

7. ongoing   (   )   8. ramp   (   )   9. outlet   (   )

10. stereotype   (   )

a．～を克服する	b．はけ口	c．国内の
d．～を成功させる，うまくやる	e．固定概念	f．傾斜台
g．危険をはらんだ	h．継続する	i．性差を表した	j．不満

2 Listening Practice 1 — First Viewing —

(Time 02:15) WEB動画 DVD

Watch the news clip and write T if the statement is true or F if it is false.

1. Skaters meet to learn new skateboard tricks every Sunday.   (   )

2. People in Ethiopia think girls should help their parents at home.   (   )

3. Sosina Challa founded the all-female skate group three years ago.   (   )

4. Many girls are busy with their jobs and have a lot of things to do in Addis Ababa.
    (   )

5. Iman Mahamud fears skateboarding and does not enjoy it.   (   )

3 Listening Practice 2

Listen to the recording and fill in the missing words.

Narrator: Every Saturday these skaters meet to learn new tricks. How to nail a landing, how to find their balance, and how to push back against gendered stereotypes.

Sosina Challa: When you being a woman or a girl, it is very hard. [1]( ) ( ) ( ) ( ) ( ) ( ) is really hard because people think that like girls should have to help their parents at their house.

Narrator: The all-female group was founded by Sosina Challa three years ago after she broke away from the non-profit Ethiopia Skate. Since then it has taught more than 150 girls to skate.

Hanna Bless: It's not really common for a girl to start skating and [2]( ) ( ) ( ) ( ) ( ), but somebody had to be the first or some group had to start, and we were the first one, and I feel honored to be part of that.

Narrator: In a country grappling with an ongoing civil war, [3]( ) ( ) ( ) ( ) can be scarce. Challa and her co-founder, Micky Asfaw, hope that they can provide a positive outlet for pent up frustrations.

grapple 取り組む

pent up うっ積した

Micky Asfaw: The girls need more attention on different types of extreme sports, so that's why the project is important for us. So there are a lot of girls in the streets with no jobs and a lot of girls who need more activities to be busy on than spending their time in bad areas and doing bad things. So we give them time here [4]( ) ( ) ( ) ( ) ( ) ( ).

35 **Iman Mahamud:** It helped me to defeat
my fears, and to not give anything
about what other people say
about me, but people say about
me being a girl and doing such stuff, which is not
40 something normal for the society. But I just enjoyed it.
It makes me happy. Even just I can't explain it.

Narrator: In this pocket of capital Addis Ababa, the girls are
⁵(   )   (   )   (   )
(   ) with claiming their place on the ramps.

④ Comprehension Check — Second Viewing —

Watch the news clip again and answer the following questions in English.

1. How many girls has Sosina Challa taught to skate?

_____

2. What do Challa and Asfaw hope they can provide?

_____

3. How does Hanna Bless feel to be one of the first girls to start skating?

_____

4. Why does Micky Asfaw think the project is important?

_____

5. What is not normal for society according to Iman Mahamud?

_____

⑤ Summary

(1-28)

Listen to the recording and complete the summary.

An all-female skateboarding group in Ethiopia faced ¹(   ). The founder,
Sosina Challa, started the group three years ago to ²(   ) girls to take up
the sport despite social pressure to ³(   ) household chores. The group
has since taught over 150 girls to skate, providing an ⁴(   ) activity to
5 hanging out in bad areas. One participant, Iman, shares that the group has helped
her ⁵(   ) her fears and not care about societal expectations that girls
should not skate.

Gender stereotypes are people's ideas about how males and females should behave based on gender. These ideas can cause problems for people
5 because they limit what they can do and make them feel unequal.

Gender stereotypes create inequality between men and women by promoting discrimination and unequal opportunities. For example, employers may use the idea
10 that women are emotional or weak to keep them from leadership roles at work. Another problem with gender stereotypes is that they promote gender-based violence. Stereotypes support ideas, such as the belief that men should be tough and not show emotions. These ideas can contribute to a culture of aggression against women and other groups. These stereotypes can also harm mental health by creating
15 unrealistic ideas. As a result, people may experience high levels of stress or depression. Furthermore, gender stereotypes pressure most people to follow how others think and act, which can lead to anxiety. They can make people unhappy because they stop them from being themselves. Lastly, gender stereotypes can prevent people from getting a good education or job. For instance, some people think
20 that only men can be good at certain jobs, such as scientists or business leaders. If employers believe this idea, they might not give women the same chances to be hired. Women may not get the same promotions at work or have the same salary. The impacts of these ideas can prevent women from reaching their full abilities.

Gender stereotypes are beliefs that can be harmful. They create inequality and
25 mental health issues. To treat everyone fairly, gender stereotypes must be challenged and overcome. By doing this, everyone can have the same chances to achieve their life goals.

(280words)

1 Vocabulary Check

Fill in the blanks with the most appropriate word from the list below.

1. The instructor was satisfied because her students started to show a (   ) degree of confidence.
2. Amelia knew how best to (   ) to the new project.
3. Team members pointed out that the manager's expectations were (   ).
4. The students strived hard to (   ) the goals given by the professor.
5. You should not (   ) your potential by thinking negatively of yourself.

> contribute   achieve   certain   unrealistic   limit

2 Comprehension Questions

Answer the following questions in English.

1. How are gender stereotypes defined?

2. Why do gender stereotypes create inequality between men and women?

3. What happens when unrealistic ideas are generated by gender stereotypes?

4. What do gender stereotypes pressure people to do?

5. What can be realized by challenging and overcoming gender stereotypes?

3 Grammar Check

Unscramble the following words and complete the sentences.

1. The last person [front, office, lock, should, leave, to, the, the] door.
   The last person [   ] door.

2. Noah said he would purchase [could, used, the, if, computer, get, he] a discount.
   Noah said he would purchase [   ] a discount.

3. The budget cut [trips, making, team, the, from, business, prevented].
   The budget cut [   ].

53

III Discussion

インターネットなどを利用し，ジェンダー・ステレオタイプについて調べましょう。ジェンダー・ステレオタイプは他人を傷つけ，不公平を生む可能性があるにもかかわらず，いまだに信じている人が多いのはなぜだと思いますか。このような固定概念をやめさせ，誰もが平等に扱われるようにするためにはどうしたら良いでしょうか。性別の固定概念の問題点，その問題の解決方法について検討し，主張，理由など自らの考えをまとめ，発表しましょう。

ジェンダー・ステレオタイプの例と その問題点について調べてみましょう。

Gender stereotype	Problems
(例) mannish 　　feminine 　　gender barriers	(例) playing sports 　　playing with toys

Discussion Topic

Why do you think some people still believe in gender stereotypes even though they can hurt others and create unfairness?

What can we do to stop these stereotypes and make sure that everyone is treated equally?

Memo

Opinion

Africa to press climate finance demands at COP26

富のレベルも気候変動に対する責任も異なる国々が，環境を守りながら経済成長を可能にする公正な解決策を見つけるために，どのように協力できるでしょうか。COP26 について考えましょう。

I Listening

1 Key Word Study — Before Watching the Video —

Match each word with its definition.

1. ambitious ( )   2. catastrophic ( )   3. curb ( )

4. drought ( )   5. flooding ( )   6. landmark ( )

7. mobilize ( )   8. obsolete ( )   9. occurrence ( )

10. pledge ( )

a．干ばつ	b．時代遅れの	c．出来事	d．野心的な
e．〜を動員する	f．重大な	g．洪水	h．壊滅的な
i．誓約	j．〜に歯止めをかける		

2 Listening Practice 1 — First Viewing —

(Time 01:46) WEB動画 🖥 **DVD**

Watch the news clip and write T if the statement is true or F if it is false.

1. The United Nations climate talks will open in Scotland. ( )

2. About 200 countries will discuss limiting CO_2 emissions. ( )

3. The Paris Agreement says $100 billion is a maximum goal. ( )

4. Sub-Saharan Africa is the most vulnerable to climate change. ( )

5. Only rich countries set targets for reducing their carbon emissions at the Paris climate talks. ( )

Narrator: It may be our last chance to curb climate change
¹( ) ( ) ( )
( ) ( ). Fresh UN climate
talks open in Scotland on Sunday. Around 200 countries
will discuss limiting carbon dioxide emissions. The
goal is to prevent the Earth from heating up more than
1.5℃ ²( ) ( ) ( )
( ). Meanwhile Africa says rich countries
are falling short of promises to pay $100 billion each
year to poor nations. The targets
need to be much more ambitious
according to the African bloc's
chief negotiator.

negotiator 交渉者

Tanguy Gahouma-Bekale: Today, this
promise has become obsolete, it
is no longer relevant, and yet
developed countries are still unable
to mobilize the funds. Our view now is that we need
to go much further, ³( ) ( )
( ) ( ) ( )
( ) under the Paris Agreement, because
the agreement says $100 billion is a minimum.

Narrator: A new UN tally says the world is heading for
catastrophic warming of 2.7℃ by 2100. July this year
⁴( ) ( ) ( )
( ) ever recorded. Sub-Saharan Africa is
the most vulnerable to these changes with severe
weather occurrences like droughts or flooding and
knock-on effects of rising sea levels and hunger. Six
years ago, at the landmark Paris climate talks nearly
every country in the world set
targets for reducing their carbon
emissions, but the sum total of
their pledges ⁵( )

Paris Agreement パリ協定
(第21回気候変動枠組条約締
約国会議（COP21）が開催
されたフランスのパリにて
2015年12月12日に採択さ
れた，気候変動抑制に関する
多国間の国際的な協定（合意）)
tally 計算

sub-Saharan Africa サハラ
砂漠より南のアフリカの地域

35   (   )   (   )   (   )

(   ) (   ). It remains to be seen if

updated pledges will be enough.

4   Comprehension Check   — Second Viewing —

Watch the news clip again and answer the following questions in English.

1. What is the goal of new UN climate talks in Scotland?

_____

2. In what way do African nations say rich countries are falling short of their promises?

_____

3. What does a new UN tally say?

_____

4. To which weather occurrences is Sub-Saharan Africa the most vulnerable?

_____

5. In what way did the total of their pledges fall short?

_____

5   Summary   CD (1-32)

Listen to the recording and complete the summary.

Around 200 countries will discuss cutting carbon dioxide [1](   ) at the fresh UN climate talks. Africa accuses rich countries of failing to pay the [2](   ) $100 billion annually to poor nations. A recent UN report warns that the world is on track to [3](   ) catastrophic warming of 2.7℃ by 2100.

5   July 2021 was the [4](   )month on record. At the Paris climate talks six years ago, most countries pledged to reduce their carbon emissions, but their combined commitments were [5](   ).

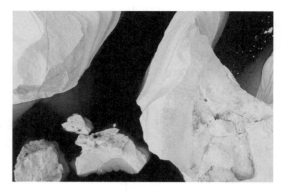

Climate change affects all countries, but determining the responsibility for the adverse effects is highly contested.

Many say that advanced countries,
5 having historically emitted more greenhouse gases, should take most of the blame for the problems they have caused. They also say these countries have more money and better technology to help reduce the effects. They point out
10 that developing countries, unlike richer ones, often face the most risk from effects such as rising sea levels. Furthermore, they must deal with extreme weather events that undermine food security, cause public health problems, and limit access to clean water. Developing countries know they need to reduce emissions, but they say their main concerns are their economies and poverty. They believe they should focus on
15 raising more money to deal with these issues. They say other countries had choices when building their economies and industries, and so it is unfair to ask poorer nations to pay for the outcomes.

However, the issue is not just one group against another. The solutions for reducing climate change need to be applied worldwide. Therefore, each country's
20 situation must be considered, such as how much money they have, their level of economic development, and importantly, how much pollution they produce. Deals such as the Paris Agreement aim to create a worldwide system. Deals help with climate issues by letting all countries work together and share funding and technology where needed.

25 All countries must play a role in reducing climate change. While it is true that developed countries are more to blame, it is a threat that has outcomes on a global scale. Evidence suggests all nations should work together and take steps to invest in a low-carbon future where they can.

(285words)

1 Vocabulary Check

Fill in the blanks with the most appropriate word from the list below.

1. Inflation has been a major (   ) of some developed countries in recent years.

2. The university is (   ) to make its campus environmentally friendly.

3. The (   ) of the drastic measure is yet to be seen.

4. The initiative was (   ) by the opposing party and failed in the end.

5. The automotive (   ) has been developing electric and hydrogen-fueled vehicles.

outcome	industry	concern	determined	undermined

2 Comprehension Questions

Answer the following questions in English.

1. Why do many people say advanced countries are more responsible for climate change?

_____

2. How do extreme weather events affect developing countries?

_____

3. What three factors of each country's situation need to be considered?

_____

4. What happens when worldwide deals are concluded?

_____

5. What terminology is used in the passage to refer to a future with lower levels of greenhouse gas?

_____

3 Grammar Check

Unscramble the following words and complete the sentences.

1. The effectiveness [policy, highly, new, doubtful, the, is, of].
   The effectiveness [   ].

2. The report [out, the, of, quality, that, air, pointed] the country is getting worse.
   The report [   ] the country is getting worse.

3. The meeting failed to reach an agreement because [nations, proposal, against, the, were, several].
   The meeting failed to reach an agreement because [
   _____].

III Discussion

インターネットなどを利用し，COP26，地球温暖化対策について調べましょう。
富のレベルも気候変動に対する責任も異なる国々が，環境を守りながら経済成長を可能
にする公正な解決策を見つけるために，どのように協力できるでしょうか。COP26で検
討されている費用負担の問題点，その問題の解決方法について検討し，主張，理由など
自らの考えをまとめ，発表しましょう。

温暖化対策についての国際会議について 調べてみましょう。

Global Warming Prevention Talks	problems
(例) Kyoto Protocol COP21 COP26	(例) target for each country is not clear

Discussion Topic

How can countries with different levels of wealth and responsibility for climate change work together to find fair solutions that protect the environment and allow for economic growth?

Memo

Opinion

Lesson 9

Tourism's gifts and woes for Santa and Sami homeland

小さな町の歴史や特色，そこに住む人々や習慣を守りながら，観光客の来訪を促し，地域経済を活性化させるには，人々や行政，観光団体はどうすれば良いのでしょうか。

Ⅰ Listening

1 Key Word Study — Before Watching the Video —

Match each word with its definition.

1. accuse	( )	2. Arctic	( )	3. cater to	( )
4. compensate	( )	5. green credentials	( )	6. differentiate	( )
7. indigenous	( )	8. lucrative	( )	9. offensive	( )
10. rush	( )				

a. 慌てる	b. 先住の	c. 魅力的な（儲かる）	d. ～を補償する
e. 北極圏の	f. ～を非難する	g. （要求など）に応じる	h. グリーン認定
i. ～を差別化する	j. 不快な		

2 Listening Practice 1 — First Viewing —

(Time 02:42) WEB動画 DVD

Watch the news clip and write T if the statement is true or F if it is false.

1. Lapland in Finland breaks new tourist records every winter. (   )
2. Customers like to do the same kind of activity wherever they come from. (   )
3. Mass tourism is an increasing advantage for the economy. (   )
4. The Sami community is an indigenous reindeer herding people in Lapland.
   (   )
5. Flying to the Arctic is eco-friendly in terms of CO_2 emissions. (   )

Listen to the recording and fill in the missing words.

Narrator: Santa Claus Village on the Arctic circle is about as close to a real-life Christmas card scene as it's possible to get. Every passing

5 winter breaks new tourism records in Finland's slice of Lapland, which for decades [1](   ) (   ) (   ) the real home of Father Christmas. Visitors, especially from Europe, stayed for an all-time high of three million

10 nights last year. And Lapland tourism is now catching on in lucrative new markets such as China.

Sanna Karkkainen: We see big differences in what activities the different customer groups like to do here. Dog-sledding and longer hikes are popular with French

15 visitors for example, British travelers are [2](   ) (   ) (   ) (   ), and the Asian tourists are most keen on seeing the Northern Lights.

Narrator: Thanks to the boom, unemployment in the town of

20 Rovaniemi is at its lowest in three decades. But for residents used to rural tranquility, mass tourism is a growing concern. Many complain of disruption and mess left behind by the thousands of visitors. Lapland's indigenous reindeer-herding Sami community accuses

25 the tourist industry of spreading offensive stereotypes of witches and shamans, and profiting [3](   ) (   ) (   ) (   ) (   ) (   ). Plus, there's the heavy emission cost of flying to the Arctic, an area

30 scientists say is heating up twice as fast as the global average.

Satu Loiro: We are very dependent on flight traffic so we are trying to communicate to tourists that they would

Lapland ラップランド地方

Northern Lights オーロラ

tranquility 静けさ

reindeer-herding トナカイを飼っている
Sami サーミ（北スカンジナビアに居住し，トナカイを移動させている土着の遊牧民族）
shaman シャーマン（霊魂との交信や病気の治療ができると信じられている宗教指導者）

35 compensate their flight when they come to Lapland and
    ⁴(   ) (   ) (   )
    (   ) (   ), use the local products.

Narrator: Valentijn Beets grew up in
Botswana but moved to Finland
40 two decades ago—and says his
thriving husky-sledding business
has been a long-term dream. He caters to more and
more eco-aware tourists, who care about animal
welfare and the green credentials of his operation.

45 **Valentijn Beets:** If you want to differentiate yourself from
your competitors or something, this is one of the ways
of doing it, and there is a growing slice of the... or a
growing group of people who actually think this is
important.

50 **Narrator:** As the days count down to Christmas, one man
insists that all the extra visitors to his grotto won't leave
him rushing to deliver all the presents—⁵(   )
(   ) (   ) (   )
(   ). The rest of Lapland's tourist industry
55 is having to learn to balance the complex and competing
interests here—without the help of magic.

husky-sledding ハスキー犬そり

grotto 洞窟

❹ Comprehension Check — Second Viewing —

WEB動画 □ DVD

Watch the news clip again and answer the following questions in English.

1. How many nights did Europeans stay in Lapland last year?

_____

2. How does the unemployment rate in Rovaniemi compare to that 30 years ago?

_____

3. How fast is the Arctic region heating up in comparison to the global average?

_____

4. What kind of tourists does Valentijn Beets cater to?

_____

5. What does the rest of Lapland's tourist industry have to learn?

_____

Listen to the recording and complete the summary.

The Santa Claus Village on the Arctic circle is a very popular tourist
[1](   ), with every winter breaking new tourism records in Finland's
Lapland region. However, Lapland's indigenous reindeer-herding Sami community
feels that the [2](   ) industry is spreading offensive stereotypes of witches
5 and shamans and [3](   ) at the expense of their ancient culture. To address
this issue, the community is urging tourists to compensate for their flight
[4](   ) and use local services and products. The rest of Lapland's tourist
industry is also trying to [5](   ) different interests without relying on
magic.

Ⅱ Reading

(1-37)

    Rural locations have always used their setting, culture, and traditions as a
chance to attract visitors and raise much-needed income for the area. But although
the local economy can benefit from the money raised, an influx of tourists has good
and bad points.

5   Mass tourism can provide a range of jobs to people who live locally. More visitors
mean there is a higher demand for products and services. This demand creates
opportunities for employment in businesses such as hotels and restaurants. The
funds gained can result in better living standards for the region. In addition, tourism
can help preserve cultural heritage. Visitors can see and learn first-hand about the
10 local traditions and way of life from those who live it. The influx of visitors can
create new opportunities for locals to teach and sell folk crafts and promote their
culture and history.

    On the other hand, mass tourism can create a number of problems. First, visitors
can cause environmental damage by littering or harming natural resources. The
15 number of people can also lead to overcrowding on public roads and trains and
greater demand for services. The result is increased costs for local people who can
no longer live in the area. They may then be forced to move away to find affordable
homes. Further, indigenous groups argue that increasing the number of tourists
leads to the commercialization of local culture and customs, creates false ideas, and
20 misrepresents the people.

    Mass tourism, then, can have both good and bad effects. Governments, tourism boards, and local communities must work together to support an industry that benefits the local people while protecting the environment and the culture of rural locations.

(277 words)

1 Vocabulary Check

Fill in the blanks with the most appropriate word from the list below.

1. Recycling is something we can do in our daily lives to help reduce ( ) impact.

2. You can ( ) invaluable experience by travelling to places which are not in the guidebooks.

3. Mia likes to spend her holidays in ( ) areas away from the bustle of city life.

4. The outdoor museum partially relies on funding from the local government to ( ) historical buildings.

5. The café is popular because it offers delicious pancakes at an ( ) price.

preserve	gain	affordable	environmental	rural

2 Comprehension Questions

Answer the following questions in English.

1. In which job sectors can we see an increase in demand as a result of mass tourism?

2. What can visitors learn about from local people?

3. What are examples of environmental damage caused by visitors?

4. What are indigenous groups concerned about?

5. Who should work together to deal with mass tourism?

3 Grammar Check

Unscramble the following words and complete the sentences.

1. Visitors [stop, encouraged, by, to, the, center, are, visitor] to register their names before hiking the trails.

   Visitors [   ] to register their names before hiking the trails.

2. Promoting the town actively on social media [to, led, increase, in, rapid, a, has] the number of tourists.

   Promoting the town actively on social media [   ] the number of tourists.

3. Michael decided to chop vegetables [boil, to, the, while, water, for, waiting].

   Michael decided to chop vegetables [   ].

Ⅲ Discussion

小さな町の歴史や特色，そこに住む人々や習慣を守りながら，観光客の来訪を促し，地域経済を活性化させるには，人々や行政，観光団体はどうすればいいのでしょうか。問題点，その解決方法について検討し，主張，理由など自らの考えをまとめ，発表しましょう。

昔からある文化と形を変えた慣習，その問題点について調べてみましょう。

Local culture	Visitors	Problems
(例) Ninja	(例) Ninja restaurant in Tokyo	(例) misunderstanding false interpretation

Discussion Topic

How can people, governments, and tourism groups encourage tourists to visit and help the local economy, while also protecting the history and the special features of small towns, the people living there, and their customs?

Memo

Opinion

Untapped potential: The Central African Republic develops its agricultural sector

投資家が資金を投じる先を
選ぶ際，途上国への投資か
ら得られる可能性のある利
益が，汚職や脆弱な法制度
などのリスクに見合うかど
うか，どのように判断すれ
ば良いでしょうか。

Ⅰ Listening

① Key Word Study　— Before Watching the Video —

Match each word with its definition.

1. conserve （　） 2. criticism （　） 3. cultivation （　）
4. deforestation （　） 5. exceptional （　） 6. fertile （　）
7. fluctuation （　） 8. governance （　） 9. plunge （　）
10. thrive （　）

a．統治	b．無謀な賭け	c．繁栄する	d．大切にする
e．栽培	f．特別な	g．変動	h．批判
i．森林破壊	j．肥沃な		

② Listening Practice 1　— First Viewing —

(Time 02:43)　WEB動画 📀 DVD

Watch the news clip and write T if the statement is true or F if it is false.

1. According to the UN, the Central African Republic is the least developed country by the UN. 　　　（　）
2. Almost the entire population is suffering from hunger and starvation. 　（　）
3. Jean-Luc Tété is a private investor who was born in the Central African Republic. 　　　（　）
4. Some critics claim that the cultivation of palm oil is harmful to the environment. 　　　（　）
5. Two thirds of the staple food cassava in the Central African Republic is imported. 　　　（　）

WEB動画 ▭ ◉ DVD ◉ CD(1-39)

Listen to the recording and fill in the missing words.

Narrator: A truck laden with commercial crops is a rare sight here. It's a paradox of the Central African Republic which the UN ranks as the second least developed country in the world. Nearly half the population is in a
5　state of food emergency despite millions of hectares of arable land. But things could be changing thanks to some private investors like Jean-Luc Tété who was born in Central African Republic. For the past four years, in the fertile region of Lobaye, this businessman has been
10　betting on what he calls "regenerative" agriculture. Based on traditional techniques, ¹(　　　　　) (　　　　　) (　　　　　) (　　　　　) (　　　　　). He sees great agribusiness potential in a country that has faced decades of armed conflict and
15　poor governance.

Jean-Luc Tété: We have available land, we have an exceptional climate, we have quite exceptional market conditions, and in fact we decided to create a champion of sustainable agriculture because ²(　　　　　)
20　(　　　　　) (　　　　　) (　　　　　) (　　　　　) an agriculture that conserves the soil and it allows us to have extremely low production costs, which are the necessary conditions to be able to start agriculture here.

25　**Narrator:** Land use is negotiated with the village chiefs. And 20 percent of profits are ³(　　　　　) (　　　　　) (　　　　　) (　　　　　) (　　　　　), some of which went
30　into building a school. But few investors have taken the plunge in this initiative. The Palme d'Or company, which is a producer of palm oil, is still the only major investor.

Raed Harriri: We've been witnessing this for years, through

arable 耕作に適する

Lobaye ロバイエ州
regenerative 再生させる

agribusiness 農業関連産業

Palme d'Or パルムドール社

69

35　food aid, which never develops the
　　sector. On the contrary, it makes
　　us lazier. It inculcates in our heads

inculcate 教え込む

　　a mentality of the assisted, the
　　people who always ⁴(　　　　) (　　　　)
40　(　　　　) (　　　　) (　　　　)
　　(　　　　). But when it's the private sector that
　　takes charge, it's something else. It's a question of
　　partnership between those who are going to invest and
　　the producers, and everyone wins.
45 **Narrator:** This investment drive is also focusing on the
　　manufacturing of processed products, such as palm oil
　　soaps, to better protect the industry, and its workers,
　　from fluctuations in the price of raw materials. But the
　　cultivation of palm oil in the region has faced criticism
50　from environmentalists, who have warned that
　　⁵(　　　　) (　　　　) (　　　　)
　　(　　　　) (　　　　) biodiversity and a
　　driver of deforestation. In a country where two thirds of
　　the food staple cassava is imported, developing this

cassava キャッサバ（南米原
産のトウダイグサ科の低木）

55　sector could help to stop people having to choose
　　between eating and thriving.

4 Comprehension Check — Second Viewing —

Watch the news clip again and answer the following questions in English.

1. How many hectares of arable land are available in the Central African Republic?

_____

2. What has Jean-Luc Tété been betting on as an investment for the past four years?

_____

3. Why did he decide to create a champion of sustainable agriculture?

_____

4. How was 20 percent of profits from land use used?

_____

5. What does Palme d'Or produce?

_____

5 Summary

Listen to the recording and complete the summary.

The United Nations has ranked the Central African Republic as the second least developed country in the world. Despite there being lots of land [1](   ) for farming, almost half of the population is experiencing a severe shortage of food. Currently, the main [2](   ) in the region is the Palme d'Or company, which

5 produces palm oil. However, there is a push to invest in the [3](   ) of processed products, like palm oil soap, to protect the industry from price changes. While this investment drive could help the economy, environmentalists have warned that palm oil production could threaten [4](   ) and cause deforestation. Developing the farming sector could help reduce the country's reliance on imported

10 food and provide better [5](   ) for the local population.

II Reading

CD(1-41)

Investing in countries that are still developing can be complex, but it also offers chances for those people who like taking risks. There are several ways to do this and some crucial points to remember. These include identifying businesses people are willing to invest in and observing the state of the countries.

5   One way to invest is to buy company shares. Buying shares is a way to profit from the company's growth while avoiding other dangers. For example, someone could buy shares in a company with a good record of selling products in many growing countries. This allows someone to benefit from the growth in these economies while also spreading money across different countries. Another way to

10 invest in poorer nations is to put money into banks and other firms that manage money. These businesses are often key in lending to local businesses and supporting growth. By investing in these groups, investors can benefit from working with stable and experienced companies. A third way to invest in poorer countries is to put money into big schemes. This means investing in plans for new energy projects,

15 such as wind or solar power. In this way, investors can make money from the growth of the markets over time as they run and maintain the projects. In addition, it is essential to consider the overall situation in countries that are the target of investment. This means considering how much corruption there is and whether a strong legal system exists.

20   Putting money into less wealthy countries allows people to make money from

their progress and offers different ways to invest. However, it is important to carefully consider the overall state of the countries where money is being risked.

(284 words)

1 Vocabulary Check

Fill in the blanks with the most appropriate word from the list below.

1. The rumor, which (   ) rapidly, turned out to be false.
2. The new marketing (   ) of the company targeted younger generations.
3. Checking the financial standing of similar businesses allows investors to (   ) successful companies.
4. The factory made great (   ) last year thanks to the introduction of new machinery.
5. The article revealed (   ) in the local government, and several officials were arrested as a result.

| identify | spread | scheme | progress | corruption |

2 Comprehension Questions

Answer the following questions in English.

1. What is a way to profit from a company's growth?

2. Why is putting money into banks and other firms that manage money a way to invest in poorer nations?

3. What are examples of big schemes given in the passage?

4. How can investors earn money from putting money into big schemes?

5. What is essential for investors to consider before making an investment?

3 Grammar Check

Unscramble the following words and complete the sentences.

1. The bank has [the, a, country, number, branches, of, across, large].

   The bank has [   ].

2. It is [students, opportunities, are, important, given, that] to engage in volunteer work while at university.

   It is [   ] to engage in volunteer

   work while at university.

3. Mr. Harris said [course, willing, was, offer, he, on, another, to] global development next semester.

   Mr. Harris said [   ] global development

   next semester.

III Discussion

投資家が資金を投じる先を選ぶ際，途上国への投資から得られる可能性のある利益が，汚職や脆弱な法制度などのリスクに見合うかどうか，どのように判断すれば良いでしょうか。途上国への投資の問題点，その問題の解決方法について検討し，主張，理由など自らの考えをまとめ，発表しましょう。

投資先の例とその問題点について
調べてみましょう。

Investment	Problems
(例) agriculture 　　natural resources mining	(例) risks in forward transaction

Discussion Topic

How can investors decide if the possible profits from investing in developing countries are worth risks such as corruption and weak legal systems, when choosing where to put their money?

Memo

Opinion

Going home: Europe starts slow return of looted African art

異なる文化圏の品々を展示・保護しながら，その品物が生まれた国の感情や権利を尊重するために，美術館はどのような公平な方法を見いだせるのでしょうか。

I Listening

1 Key Word Study ◀ – Before Watching the Video –

Match each word with its definition.

1. artifact （　） 2. broadly 　（　） 3. dedicated （　）

4. legacy （　） 5. momentum （　） 6. racism 　（　）

7. sculpture （　） 8. subsequent （　） 9. throne 　（　）

10. troop 　（　）

a．軍隊	b．美術品	c．〜専門の	d．王座
e．勢い	f．それに続く	g．遺産	h．広く
i．彫刻	j．人種差別		

2 Listening Practice 1 ◀ – First Viewing –

(Time 02:31)　WEB動画 DVD

Watch the news clip and write T if the statement is true or F if it is false.

1. France is preparing to receive 26 looted works of art from Benin. 　　（　）

2. Totem statues and the throne of King Behanzin were looted when colonial troops ransacked the palace in 1892. 　　（　）

3. Cambridge University returned a Benin bronze statue looted a century ago. （　）

4. The cockerel was looted from the former kingdom of Nigeria. 　　（　）

5. The University of Aberdeen returned an object taken from the continent during colonial rule. 　　（　）

Listen to the recording and fill in the missing words.

Narrator: The return of looted African art from Europe is gaining momentum. France is preparing to send back 26 looted works of art to Benin. British universities formally handed back artworks to African governments.

5 On Wednesday, French President Emmanuel Macron visited the exhibit from the Kingdom of Dahomey, which is present-day Benin. These royal treasures from erstwhile capital city Abomey have been kept at the Quai Branly Museum, dedicated to African art, in

10 Paris.

Emmanuel Macron: As you can see, this restitution is more than just restitution. It's [1]( )
( ) ( )

15 ( ) that should allow us to strengthen our ties, to create new opportunities for discussions, meetings, and projects. And that is perfectly consistent with what we wish to do more broadly.

Narrator: Among the works are totem statues as well as the

20 throne of King Behanzin, Dahomey's last independent rule. They were looted when colonial troops ransacked the palace in 1892. Macron will
[2]( ) ( )
( ) ( )

25 to Benin's President Patrice Talon on November 9. Also on Wednesday, Cambridge University returned to Nigeria a bronze statue looted a century ago. It is the first British institution to return an object
[3]( ) ( )

30 ( ) ( )
( ) ( )
( ) ( ).

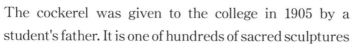

The cockerel was given to the college in 1905 by a student's father. It is one of hundreds of sacred sculptures

---

loot 略奪する

Benin ベニン（アフリカ西部の共和国）

Kingdom of Dahomey ダホメ王国（現在のアフリカ・ベナンにあったアフリカ人の王国）
erstwhile かつての
Abomey アボメイ（ベニン南部の都市）
Quai Branly Museum ケ・ブランリ美術館

restitution 返還

totem トーテム

King Behanzin ベハンジン王（ダホメの王）
ransack 荒らし回る

Patrice Talon パトリス・タロン（ベニンの大統領）

cockerel 雄鶏

35 and carvings known as the Benin Bronzes which were looted from the former kingdom of Benin in southern Nigeria.

carvings 彫刻

Abba Isa Tijan: We are very happy to see that this artifact,
40 which has been away from Nigeria for decades, is in good shape, excellent shape. And by the time
   ⁴(   ) (   ) (   )
   (   ) (   ) (   )
   Nigeria, people in Nigeria will be extremely excited.

45 **Narrator:** Just a day after Scotland's University of Aberdeen held a similar ceremony. Anti-racism movements in 2020 and the subsequent questioning of colonial legacy gave new drive to the campaign for the return of looted artworks to Africa. Since then, ⁵(   )
50 (   ) (   ) (   ) have said they plan to hand looted African treasures back too. According to experts, as much as 90 percent of Africa's heritage is currently outside the
55 continent.

4 Comprehension Check /– Second Viewing –/

WEB動画 DVD

Watch the news clip again and answer the following questions in English.

1. What is becoming popular in Europe?

_____

2. What treasures have been kept at the Quai Branly Museum in Paris?

_____

3. What does restitution mean according to President Macron?

_____

4. What did a student's father give to Cambridge's Jesus College in 1905?

_____

5. What percentage of African treasures is outside the continent?

_____

Listen to the recording and complete the summary.

France is giving back 26 artworks taken during a [1](   ) raid in 1892 to Benin, and the formal [2](   ) will take place on November 9. Cambridge University has also returned a bronze [3](   ) that was looted a century ago to Nigeria, which is part of a [4](   ) of sculptures called the Benin
5   Bronzes that were taken in 1897. The people of Nigeria will be very [5](   ) to see the statue returned to their country after many years. Anti-racism movements in 2020 and the subsequent questioning of colonial legacy gave new drive to the campaign for the return of looted artworks to Africa.

II Reading

(2-04)

Since the mid-20th century, there has been a growing debate about whether museums in developed countries should keep items taken during colonial times.
5   Many of these items were acquired through theft or other forms of colonial looting. More people now believe that keeping culturally important objects from their sources is wrong. However, returning treasures and artworks is a complex
10   issue, with arguments for and against it.

On the one hand, museums say they protect and preserve cultural items for future generations. They take care of treasures and keep them in the best conditions. Museums argue that their role is challenging for countries that might need more resources, skills, or infrastructure to look after fragile and valuable artifacts. They
15   also say that museums help promote other cultures by showing art and history from different countries to a broader audience. Museums believe that returning these items would take away the chance for people to see and learn from them.

On the other hand, some argue that returning artifacts is about doing what is right and following the law. They see these items as a way to make up for the
20   damage and losses of the past. They believe that giving back items can help recognize and admit past wrongs. They also point to international law, which says that items stolen during conflict should be returned to their rightful owners.

Ultimately, the decision to return treasures and artworks to their original countries will depend on each case. Various factors will be considered, including the
25 item's importance, the situation in the country it came from, and whether those receiving the item can take care of it properly. This will help ensure that institutions make the right decision for each artifact.

(286 words)

1 Vocabulary Check

Fill in the blanks with the most appropriate word from the list below.

1. The museum has a (   ) security system to protect the artifacts.
2. The vase was so (   ) that the curators had to handle it with extreme care.
3. The library recently (   ) valuable books from a collector.
4. Many artifacts were brought to Europe from Africa during the (   ) period.
5. The librarian immediately (   ) the book even though the customer had mentioned a wrong title.

acquired	recognized	complex	fragile	colonial

2 Comprehension Questions

Answer the following questions in English.

1. How were some artifacts collected during colonial times?

2. Why do museums argue that some countries may not be able to look after valuable artifacts?

3. How can museums promote other cultures?

4. What does international law state about stolen artifacts?

5. What factors should be considered in deciding whether to return the artifacts to their original countries?

3 Grammar Check

Unscramble the following words and complete the sentences.

1. The teacher decided [truth, keep, the, her, to, students, from] so that they would not feel worried.

   The teacher decided [_____] so that they would not feel worried.

2. The professor asked the students [they, learned, topic, had, about, what, the] in the previous semester.

   The professor asked the students [_____] in the previous semester.

3. Kelly was not sure [she, join, event, the, whether, or, should] not.

   Kelly was not sure [_____]not.

Ⅲ Discussion

インターネットなどを利用し，植民地時代の財宝，文化財の所有権について調べましょう。異なる文化圏の品々を展示・保護しながら，その品物が生まれた国の感情や権利を尊重するために，美術館はどのような公平な方法を見いだせるのでしょうか。植民地時代の財宝，文化財所有の問題点，その問題の解決方法について検討し，主張，理由など自らの考えをまとめ，発表しましょう。

問題を抱える美術品や芸術品について 調べてみましょう。

Artifacts in Museums	Problems
(例) British Museum	(例) stolen artifacts from colonies

Discussion Topic

How can museums find a fair way to both display and protect items from different cultures while also respecting the feelings and rights of the countries where the items originally came from?

Memo

Opinion

Torfaera, the motor sport captivating Iceland

バンジージャンプやスカイダイビングなど，リスクを楽しむエクストリームスポーツに参加したいですか。危険を伴うスポーツに挑戦することの利点と，それに伴う身体的な危険性をどのように考えますか。

I Listening

1 Key Word Study — Before Watching the Video —

Match each word with its definition.

1. competitor ( )　　2. exhaust ( )　　3. financing ( )

4. keen to ( )　　5. organizer ( )　　6. progressive ( )

7. scarce ( )　　8. spectator ( )　　9. steep ( )

10. terrain ( )

a．地形	b．険しい	c．観客	d．主催者
e．進歩的な	f．競技者	g．少ない	h．資金
i．排気ガス	j．熱心に〜したがる		

2 Listening Practice 1 — First Viewing —

(Time 01:58) WEB動画 DVD

Watch the news clip and write T if the statement is true or F if it is false.

1. The Formula Offroad or Torfaera takes place on an Icelandic mountain. ( )

2. Torfaera began when Icelandic police officers showed off their vehicles. ( )

3. The first championship was held in 1965. ( )

4. Torfaera cars cost from 40,000 to 120,000 dollars. ( )

5. The number of sponsors grew in 2008 and made financing easier. ( )

Narrator: On this Icelandic mountain, drivers are testing their machines and their mettle. This is "Formula Offroad," or Torfaera—Icelandic for "difficult driving." [1]( ) ( ) ( ) ( ) ( ) steep slopes, winning points for passing gates and losing them for stopping. For many drivers, just finishing the course is more important than winning.

Haukur Einarsson: I have to be really progressive and thinking [2]( ) ( ) ( ) ( ) and try to choose the best way to drive. And maybe it's working or maybe not.

Narrator: Torfaera began in the 1960s [3]( ) ( ) ( ) ( ) ( ) ( ), when Icelandic rescue workers began to show off their vehicles on hilly terrain. The first championship took place in 1965 and has since spread to other Nordic countries and the US.

Tryggvi Thórdarson: The enjoyment is the excitement, hearing the noise and seeing people sort of trying the impossible. Some of them actually make it happen.

Narrator: Cars cost between 40,000 and 120,000 dollars, so drivers try to [4]( ) ( ) ( ) by picking safe routes along the course. But with the rough terrain, organizers still have to keep an eye on safety.

Kristján Sæmundsson: We often have fires. We have hot liquids running on exhaust and everything, so we have to [5]( ) ( ) ( ) ( ) ( ) ( ). And

Icelandic アイスランドの (語)

mettle 度胸
Formula Offroad フォーミュラ・オフロード
Torfaera トルファエラ

Nordic 北欧の

83

35　as you've seen today often, they roll over in difficult places, so we have to rescue them out safely and always make the drivers and the spectators safe.

40　**Narrator:** With the 2008 financial crisis, sponsors grew scarce, making financing more difficult. But here, Torfaera still draws in competitors looking to test their machines and spectators keen to watch them try.

4 Comprehension Check — Second Viewing —

Watch the news clip again and answer the following questions in English.

1. What does the word "torfaera" mean in the Icelandic language?

_____

2. What is more important for the drivers than winning?

_____

3. How and when did Torfaera begin?

_____

4. What is the enjoyment for Tryggvi Thórdarson?

_____

5. How do the drivers try to avoid damaging their expensive cars?

_____

5 Summary

(2-07)

Listen to the recording and complete the summary.

This is a motorsport called Formula Offroad or Torfaera in Icelandic, which means "difficult driving." Drivers [1](   ) by driving up and down steep slopes and earn points for passing gates while losing them for stopping. For many drivers, simply finishing the course is more important than [2](   ).

5　Torfaera began in the 1960s as a way to raise funds, with Icelandic rescue workers showcasing their [3](   ) on hilly terrain. The cars used in the sport can cost between $40,000 and $120,000, so drivers try to avoid [4](   ) them by picking safe routes along the course. In difficult places, cars can roll over, so organizers always make sure to [5](   ) the drivers and keep both drivers

10　and spectators safe.

Extreme sports, like skydiving, mountain biking, and snowboarding, include activities with physical or mental risks. People often enjoy the fun and
5 thrill these sports provide. But what motivates them to face real danger and potential harm or injury?

The first reason is the sensation these activities create. Many people love the excitement of risky adventures. When
10 they participate in daring sports, it releases endorphins, brain chemicals that make them feel joyful. These sports let people escape their everyday lives and experience something thrilling. Second, people join extreme sports to take on challenges. Adventurous people want to push their mental and physical limits. They believe facing challenges helps them grow and become better people. Overcoming formidable
15 obstacles in extreme sports feels satisfying and rewarding. The third reason is the sense of community extreme sports offer. Participants build strong relationships with others who share their interests. They often join group events, like competitions, which help them make friends and feel like they belong. Being part of a community with a shared passion is enjoyable. Lastly, some enjoy extreme sports because they
20 can face and conquer their fears. For many, the thrill is not just participating but overcoming challenges. They do not give up and keep pushing themselves to achieve their goals, no matter how scary they seem.

Extreme sports give people a unique chance to experience thrills, test their limits, compete with others, and do something genuinely exciting. What some might
25 believe a crazy pastime is for other participants a chance to push their boundaries, make lasting connections, and conquer their fears in a fun, supportive environment.

(265 words)

1 Vocabulary Check

Fill in the blanks with the most appropriate word from the list below.

1. The climber finally (   ) Mt. Everest last year.
2. Bungee jumping is definitely not for those who have a (   ) of heights.

3. Alex decided to (   ) in the swimming event with her classmates.
4. The annual music event brings many people to the small (   ).
5. The coach (   ) the team by setting an additional goal.

| community | fear | participate | motivated | conqured |

2 Comprehension Questions
Answer the following questions in English.

1. What is the definition of extreme sports?

_____

2. What do endorphins do?

_____

3. What do those who take part in extreme sports for the challenge look for?

_____

4. Why can extreme sports offer a sense of community?

_____

5. How do people who enjoy extreme sports try to overcome challenges?

_____

3 Grammar Check
Unscramble the following words and complete the sentences.

1. Supporting a sports team can [a, to, belonging, provide, of, sense] the fan community.
   Supporting a sports team can [   ] the fan community.

2. Spectators were impressed [handled, coach, situation, how, by, the, the, difficult].
   Spectators were impressed [   ].

3. Our friendly staff [learn, help, will, how, you, snowboard, to] even if it is your first time.
   Our friendly staff [   ] even if it is your first time.

III Discussion

インターネットなどを利用し，危険を伴うスポーツ，危険なことにあえて挑戦することについて調べましょう。危険を伴うスポーツや危険なことに挑戦することの問題点，その問題の解決方法について検討し，主張，理由など自らの考えをまとめ，発表しましょう。

危険を伴うスポーツとその問題点について調べてみましょう。

Risky Sports	Problems
(例) Formula Offroad	(例) often have fires

Discussion Topic

How do the benefits of participating in extreme sports weigh against the physical risks and dangers involved?

Do you think the overall experience of taking part in extreme sports is a healthy free time activity?

Memo

Opinion

_____

_____

_____

_____

New Zealand outlines plans to tax livestock burps and farts

政府は，企業に問題を起こさず，人々の生活費をより高額にすることなく，公共サービスのために増税し，所得をより平等にするための適切なバランスをどのようにすれば見つけられるでしょうか。

I Listening

1 Key Word Study — Before Watching the Video —

Match each word with its definition.

1. criticize ( ) 2. dairy ( ) 3. emit ( )

4. enhance ( ) 5. incentive ( ) 6. initiative ( )

7. offset ( ) 8. sufficient ( ) 9. unveil ( )

10. urine ( )

a．取り組み	b．尿	c．〜を発表する	d．乳製品の
e．十分な	f．奨励金	g．〜を相殺する	h．〜を強化する
i．〜を排出する	j．〜を批判する		

2 Listening Practice 1 — First Viewing —

(Time 02:07) WEB動画 DVD

Watch the news clip and write T if the statement is true or F if it is false.

1. Prime Minister Jacinda Ardern announced a sheep and cow burp tax to reduce greenhouse gas emissions. ( )

2. The new tax is a step toward cutting greenhouse gases in New Zealand. ( )

3. Sheep are responsible for the largest gas emissions in New Zealand. ( )

4. Greenpeace also thinks the new tax plan is helpful and agrees to it. ( )

5. Christine Rose thinks this initiative is sufficient to address the climate emergency. ( )

Narrator: New Zealand has unveiled a world first—a sheep and cow burp tax to curb emissions. Prime Minister Jacinda Ardern announced the levy on Tuesday as a step towards cutting the country's greenhouse gases.

5 Farmers will have to pay for gas emissions from their animals—such as methane from burps and farts and nitrous oxide in urine. Ardern said farmers ¹(   ) (   ) (   ) (   ) (   ) (   )

10 (   ) by charging more [for] climate-friendly products.

Jacinda Ardern: Importantly, all money raised from charges on emissions will be recycled back into the

15 system to fund further research, tools and technology, as well as farmer incentives ²(   ) (   ) (   ) (   ) (   ) (   ).

Narrator: New Zealand has a population of 5 million people,

20 but over 6 million beef and dairy cattle. Gases emitted by the farm animals are some of the country's biggest emissions. The opposition and conservatives say the plan would actually increase worldwide emissions if farmers sell up and instead move to countries that are

25 ³(   ) (   ) (   ) (   ) (   ). Farming groups are outraged.

Kate Acland: [If] farmers are going to be paying a price for

30 their emissions, we should be recognized for all of the sequestrations that are happening on our farm.

Andrew Hoggard: Those farmers will, you know, be under more pressure, their profits are under pressure, they'll look to, you know... they'll reach a point where

burp げっぷ

levy 課税

methane メタンガス
fart おなら
nitrous oxide 亜酸化窒素

[for] 映像音声にはないが，文法的に付加した。

outraged 激怒した

[if] 映像音声にはないが，文法的に付加した。

sequestration 仮差し押さえ

35   they're saying, we're out of here.

⁴(   ) (   )

(   ) (   )

(   ) (   )

(   ) will be generally offshore firms that

40   are buying up for carbon credits to offset their CO_2 emissions.

Narrator: Ardern believes the plan will enhance the New Zealand export brand. But Greenpeace has also criticized the tax, saying it misses the mark.

45 **Christine Rose:** [This] initiative actually sends the wrong signals to the wrong sector and isn't sufficient to address the climate emergency that we're in.

[This] 映像音声にはないが, 文法的に付加した。

50 **Narrator:** The government is hoping to ⁵(   )

(   ) (   ) (   )

(   ) next year and [it] could come into force by 2025.

[it] 映像音声にはないが, 文法的に付加した。

4 Comprehension Check — Second Viewing —

WEB動画 / DVD

Watch the news clip again and answer the following questions in English.

1. What would a new tax in New Zealand require farmers to pay for?

2. How will the farmers benefit from the tax?

3. How many people and cattle are living in New Zealand?

4. What does Prime Minister Ardern believe the plan will enhance?

5. What is the government hoping for regarding this new tax?

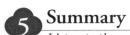

⑤ Summary

CD(2-11)

Listen to the recording and complete the summary.

Prime Minister Jacinda Ardern announced a new measure on Tuesday to decrease the greenhouse gas emissions of New Zealand. This involves farmers paying for the emissions produced by their animals, including methane released through burps and farts. Importantly, all the money ^{1}(   ) from these emission charges will
5 be reinvested into the system. This reinvestment will support further research, development of tools, and technology, and provide incentives for farmers. The emissions from farm animals ^{2}(   ) significantly to the country's overall emissions. However, critics from the opposition argue that the plan might have ^{3}(   ) consequences. They fear that if farmers are burdened by these
10 charges and decide to sell their farms and move to countries with less efficient food production, it could ^{4}(   ) lead to an increase in global emissions. This would put more pressure on these farmers as their profits are already strained. Eventually, they might reach a point where they feel ^{5}(   ) to leave.

Ⅱ Reading

CD(2-12)

Raising taxes has positive and negative effects on a country's economy and people. Taxation helps governments to collect money to pay for public services, build infrastructure, and address social issues. However,
5 increasing taxes does not happen without problems.

One advantage of raising taxes is the increased revenue for the government. The money can fund essential public services such as transport or education. A country with many older people might need more
10 services to support healthcare and a pension system. Raising taxes ensures that these services are well-

funded and help those who need them. Additionally, raising taxes can make income more equal by charging a higher rate for wealthier people. By raising taxes for the rich, governments can use the money to invest in social programs that are helpful for
15 lower-income families. Programs might include cheaper college fees, free school meals, or smaller class sizes. It could also include better public transport, childcare facilities, or job training. However, increasing taxes may also create problems.

Higher taxes can discourage investment, as individuals and businesses may have less money to reinvest in the economy. Not having enough money can slow down the
20 economy because fewer businesses open, and current ones might be cautious about hiring. Furthermore, higher taxes will cause the prices of items and services to go up. In that case, the cost of living also increases for everyone.

Raising taxes can have both positive and negative effects. Increased taxes can generate revenue to fund public services and reduce income inequality. They can
25 also discourage investment and increase the cost of living. Governments must always balance the effects to minimize the disadvantages when making tax decisions.

(276 words)

1 Vocabulary Check

Fill in the blanks with the most appropriate word from the list below.

1. Jerome was tasked with assessing the (   ) situation of the market.
2. The investment plan (   ) potential gain and risk.
3. The technology company (   ) start-ups and also offers financial advice.
4. Sophie is (   ) when it comes to taking on a new challenge.
5. The online shopping site (   ) a shipping fee for international orders.

charges	funds	balances	current	cautious

2 Comprehension Questions

Answer the following questions in English.

1. What can governments do through taxation?

   _____

2. What might a country with many older people need?

   _____

3. How can raising taxes make incomes more equal?

   _____

4. What are some examples of social programs for lower-income families mentioned in the passage?

   _____

5. Why can higher taxes discourage investment?

   _____

Unscramble the following words and complete the sentences.

1. Lily enjoys [having, get, morning, early, not, the, up, to, in] after she started to live near the campus.

   Lily enjoys [   ] after she started to live near the campus.

2. Kyoto is a popular tourist destination because [area, history, is, with, an, a, it, rich] and culture.

   Kyoto is a popular tourist destination because [

       ] and culture.

3. The welcoming environment of the dormitory [first, effects, students, on, had, positive, year].

   The welcoming environment of the dormitory [

                   ].

III Discussion

インターネットなどを利用し，新たな税金制度について調べましょう。政府は，企業に問題を起こさず，人々の生活費をより高額にすることなく，公共サービスのために増税し，所得をより平等にするための適切なバランスをどのようにすれば見つけられるでしょうか。税金制度の問題点，その問題の解決方法について検討し，主張，理由など自らの考えをまとめ，発表しましょう。

最近の税金制度とその問題点について調べてみましょう。

Recent tax system	Problems
(例) fart tax	(例) unfair

Discussion Topic

How can governments find the right balance between raising taxes to pay for public services and making incomes more equal, without causing problems for businesses and making life more expensive for people?

Memo

Opinion

Lesson 14

Poverty and activism combine in Chad street theater

音楽や詩を一緒に楽しむことは，異なる背景を持つ人々がお互いをよりよく理解し，尊重することにどのように役立つのでしょうか？　富の不平等と社会的，文化的排斥について考えましょう。

I Listening

1 Key Word Study — Before Watching the Video —

Match each word with its definition.

1. accessible   (   )   2. accompany   (   )   3. discipline   (   )

4. exile   (   )   5. makeshift   (   )   6. marvelous   (   )

7. recite   (   )   8. repertoire   (   )   9. torch   (   )

10. xylophone   (   )

a．亡命	b．〜の伴奏をする	c．レパートリー
d．〜を朗読する	e．木琴	f．入手できる g．聖火
h．仮設の	i．素晴らしい	j．学問分野

2 Listening Practice 1 — First Viewing —

(Time 02:35) WEB動画 📺 💿 DVD

Watch the news clip and write T if the statement is true or F if it is false.

1. Chagoua district is a working–class neighborhood in N'Djamena, Chad.   (   )

2. Bonaventure Madjitoubangar is reciting a poem written by an African writer.

(   )

3. Eighty percent of the people in Chad can read and write.   (   )

4. Bonaventure's recitals are always accompanied by the sound of the *koundou* which is known as an African xylophone.   (   )

5. Chad has its own theaters and cinemas now.   (   )

Bonaventure Madjitoubagar: Welcome, this is a reading and a journey in the heart of Chagoua district!

Narrator: Theater and music have come to this working-class neighborhood for a day in N'Djamena, the capital of Chad. Among the bricks and makeshift houses, Bonaventure Madjitoubangar is reciting a poem. His repertoire is mostly African writers. His performance gives their works new life, and ¹( ) ( ) ( ) ( ). In a country where only 20 percent of the population can read and write, Bonaventure is on a mission.

Chagoua シャグア地区

N'Djamena ヌジャメナ(チャドの首都)
Chad チャド (アフリカ中北部の共和国)

Bonaventure Madjitoubagar: Culture must be accessible to everyone. If we want to have a marvelous world, a harmonious world, everyone should be ²( ) ( ) ( ) ( ) ( ), to be able to dream together. Without culture, we can't even begin to develop.

Narrator: This day's reading is a poem by Chadian author Nimrod Bena Djangrang. It tells the story of his exile during the civil war in the 1980's.

Chadian チャドの
Nimrod Bena Djangrang チャドの作家

Walter Houlmbaye: I came to listen to what he is saying, and I really enjoy him performing.

Narrator: Bonaventure Madjitoubangar has been reciting on the streets for six years. And he's always accompanied by the sound of the *koundou*. ³( ) ( ) ( ) ( ) the balafon is also known as an African xylophone.

koundou チャドの木琴

balafon 西アフリカの木琴

Bonaventure Madjitoubagar: The *koundou* is part of me, it is my identity, it accompanies me, and what is beautiful about theater is that you can't do it alone. Theater relies

35 on other disciplines. And other perspectives also enrich what I do in the theater. So, it becomes a collaboration and at the same time, it speaks to your identity, and everyone can

40 recognize themselves in it.

Narrator: Bonaventure regularly organizes workshops for the neighborhood children to share his love of art and theater. With great success.

Antoinette Nojidemgen: If he is not there, our children cry.

45 Because every time, [4](   ) (   ) (   ) (   ) (   ), he brings the children together, he gives them drawings, he teaches the children to play, and to draw. I would like it to continue like that for our children and the

50 young people of the neighborhood.

Narrator: At the moment Chad does not have its own theater or cinema. Bonaventure had to train in Burkina Faso. The plan is to pass on the torch, so that [5](   ) (   ) (   ) (   )

55 (   ) the art here. At home.

Burkina Faso ブルキナファソ (アフリカ西部の独立国)

 4 **Comprehension Check** ⟍ – Second Viewing – ⟋

WEB動画 💻📀 DVD

Watch the news clip again and answer the following questions in English.

1. Where is Bonaventure reciting a poem?

_____

2. What does the story by Nimrod Bean Djangrang tell?

_____

3. What does theater rely on according to Bonaventure?

_____

4. Why does Bonaventure regularly organize workshops?

_____

5. Where did Bonaventure receive training?

_____

Listen to the recording and complete the summary.

In the working-class neighborhood of N'Djamena, the capital city of Chad, theater and music have arrived for a day. Bonaventure Madjitoubangar is ¹(   ) a poem. He mostly chooses poems by African writers. His performance brings new life to their works and offers ²(   ) a new experience. Bonaventure regularly hosts workshops for neighborhood children to ³(   ) his love of art and theater. Every two or three months, he brings the children together, gives them drawings, and ⁴(   ) them to play and draw. Antoinette hopes that this will ⁵(   ) for the children and young people in the neighborhood.

II Reading

Music and poetry play a vital role in keeping cultural history alive. They help people express a group's feelings, beliefs, and values. If culture is passed
5 on, future generations can know where they come from and maintain their ancestors' cultural traditions.

These art forms play a role in shaping the identity of people and their communities. They help to connect them
10 with their cultural roots and make them feel like they belong somewhere. By learning about and taking part in traditional music and poetry, people can develop a strong link to their history and feel greater pride in their identity. They remember the people who came before them and think about the challenges they faced. They can also remember what was important to those people and what they valued. Music and
15 poetry can also bring a community closer together. When people come together to perform or listen to traditional arts, they share a special experience that does not depend on social status, money, or politics. This shared experience promotes greater understanding and respect between people and their communities. It can be crucial in creating a more peaceful and friendly society. Lastly, they can promote
20 understanding between people from different cultures. When people listen to the music and poetry of others, they can learn more about different ways of thinking, beliefs, and ways of life. Learning about differences can give people more respect for

the difficulties in life that others may face.

Sharing the culture of music and poetry is very important. By keeping these art
25 forms alive, future generations can better understand their history, feel closer to
their culture, foster a sense of unity, and help people understand and respect each
other.

(282 words)

1 Vocabulary Check
Fill in the blanks with the most appropriate word from the list below.

1. Traditional poems often contain messages from the (　　　　　　).
2. Juliet played a (　　　　　　) role in the village festival.
3. Regional organizations promote (　　　　　　) in the area.
4. Bowing is a way to show (　　　　　　) to others.
5. The conflict between the two towns was solved in a (　　　　　　) manner.

| crucial | respect | unity | ancestors | peaceful |

2 Comprehension Questions
Answer the following questions in English.

1. What do music and poetry help people express?

_____

2. What can people do by learning about and taking part in traditional music and poetry?

_____

3. How can music and poetry bring a community closer together?

_____

4. How can music and poetry promote understanding between people from different cultures?

_____

5. What are the merits of keeping music and poetry alive for future generations?

_____

3 Grammar Check

Unscramble the following words and complete the sentences.

1. The researcher [visiting, gathered, customs, on, by, data, traditional] small communities in the mountains.

   The researcher [   ] small communities in the mountains.

2. Tourists had an opportunity to hear stories [village, people, who, lived, the, from, in, had] for many years.

   Tourists had an opportunity to hear stories [   ] for many years.

3. Alpaca sweaters are ideal [a, on, for, yourself, cold, warm, keeping] winter day.

   Alpaca sweaters are ideal [   ] winter day.

III Discussion

インターネットなどを利用し，富の不平等と社会的，文化的排斥の問題について調べましょう。音楽や詩を一緒に楽しむことは，異なる背景を持つ人々がお互いをよりよく理解し，尊重することにどのように役立つのでしょうか？　異なる背景を持つ人々がお互いをよりよく理解する上での問題点，その問題の解決方法について検討し，主張，理由など自らの考えをまとめ，発表しましょう。

富の不平等の例とその問題点について
調べてみましょう。

Poverty	Problems
(例) GINI index	(例) gap between rich and poor

Discussion Topic

How does enjoying music and poetry together help people from different backgrounds understand and respect each other better?

Memo

Opinion

Lesson 15

Rwandan company transforms gas from "killer lake" into electricity

石油やガスの掘削によるリスクから環境や人々の健康を守りながら，必要なエネルギーを確保するにはどうしたらよいでしょうか。風力発電や太陽光発電は，この問題の解決になるでしょうか。

I Listening

1 Key Word Study — Before Watching the Video —

Match each word with its definition.

1. accumulate ( )　　2. deplete ( )　　3. erupt ( )

4. ironically ( )　　5. lava ( )　　6. parallel ( )

7. suffocate ( )　　8. thermal plant ( )　　9. trigger ( )

10. volcanic ( )

a. 火力発電所	b. ～を使い尽くす	c. ～を引き起こす
d. ～を窒息させる	e. 溶岩	f. 並行　　g. 噴火する
h. 皮肉なことに	i. 蓄積する	j. 火山の

2 Listening Practice 1 — First Viewing —

(Time 02:28) WEB動画 DVD

Watch the news clip and write T if the statement is true or F if it is false.

1. Lake Kivu lies between Rwanda and the Democratic Republic of the Congo. ( )

2. There are three so-called killer lakes existing in Rwanda. ( )

3. A limnic eruption would create big waves at surface. ( )

4. Nyiragongo erupted last year, pushing a second wave of lava deep into the earth, under the lake. ( )

5. KivuWatt is a thermal plant and is considered a polluting source of energy. ( )

Narrator: Lake Kivu's vast waters form the border between Rwanda and the Democratic Republic of the Congo. And in the middle lies

5   a power plant that creates electricity from deadly gas. Methane and carbon dioxide have accumulated over thousands of years during volcanic eruptions of Mount Nyiragongo. Two million lives are at risk if the gas were to escape to the surface. That is why it is called

10 the "killer lake." Only two other such lakes exist in the world, both in Cameroon.

François Darchambeau: [1](   ) (   )
(   ) (   ) (   )
(   ) (   ) is that we have over

15 saturation of gas in the water and that it may trigger what we call a limnic eruption, which would create

waves, tsunami at surface and so on, and in the 80's in the Cameroon lakes, it killed more than 1,000

20 people. So we don't want that it happens here.

Narrator: And it is not a theoretic threat. Last year Nyiragongo erupted again, pushing a second wave of lava deep into the earth, under the lake itself. Engineers

25 considered a shutdown of the KivuWatt power plant. But [2](   ) (   ) (   )
(   ) (   ) (   ) risk into an opportunity.

François Darchambeau: Removing this gas, if it's done

30 correctly may help to reduce the risk of a limnic eruption. And of course, if when using this gas,
[3](   ) (   ) (   )
(   ) (   ) (   ) to develop by, for example, producing electricity, then we

Lake Kivu キブ湖（コンゴとルワンダの間の中央アフリカの山の湖）
Rwanda ルワンダ
Democratic republic of Congo コンゴ民主共和国

methane メタン

Mount Nyiragongo ニーラゴンゴ山（アフリカ中部コンゴ民主共和国の東境部の活火山）

Cameroon カメルーン

saturation 飽和（状態）

tsunami 津波

theoretic 理論の

KivuWatt power plant キブワット発電所

35 have two chances from one threat.

Narrator: KivuWatt provides around 30 percent of Rwanda's annual electricity. Ironically, the operators say [4](   ) (   ) (   ) (   ) (   ).

40 **Priysham Nundah:** KivuWatt is five to six times less polluting in terms of carbon emission to a traditional or conventional power plant. So, I would say why we are burning with gas here, even if it is a thermal plant, it's still considered as a clean source of energy.

45 **Narrator:** Experts say it will take centuries to deplete the massive underwater reserves. Basically, [5](   ) (   ) (   ) (   ). But in parallel, the

50 threat of death. Riverside residents tell of swimmers disappearing in Lake Kivu's depths—suffocated by the gas or pulled under.

4 Comprehension Check — Second Viewing —

Watch the news clip again and answer the following questions in English.

1. What kind of deadly gas does the power plant in Lake Kivu use to create electricity?

_____

2. Why is Lake Kivu called the "killer lake"?

_____

3. What was the result of a limnic eruption in the 80s in Cameroon?

_____

4. How much electricity does KivuWatt provide annually?

_____

5. How eco-friendly is Kivuwatt in terms of carbon emissions?

_____

5 Summary

Listen to the recording and complete the summary.

Lake Kivu, which serves as the border between Rwanda and the Democratic Republic of Congo, is home to a power plant that [1]( ) electricity using deadly gas. If this gas were to [2]( ) to the surface, it could put the lives of two million people at risk. The danger with this type of lake is that it may contain an [3]( ) amount of gas, which could trigger a massive explosion of gas to the surface, called a limnic eruption. Such an eruption could create waves, tsunamis, and other [4]( ), as it did in Cameroon in the 1980s, killing more than 1,000 people. Removing this gas, if done correctly, could reduce the [5]( ) of a limnic eruption.

II Reading

Oil and gas drilling is vital for the world's energy needs, providing fuel for cars, heating, and generating electricity. However, this process also has many risks for the environment and people's health, which cannot be ignored.

One significant risk is spills and leaks. These can happen at any time during drilling, from exploring the ground to moving the resources. Spills release harmful chemicals and pollution into the air, land, and water. The release adversely affects ecosystems and can cause health problems for animals and people. Cleaning up oil spills can be complex, costly, and lead to long-term environmental damage. Another danger is earthquakes caused by fracking. Fracking uses high-pressure liquids to break rocks and release natural gas. These earthquakes can harm buildings and homes, risking people's safety. Drilling also leads to air pollution and an increase in greenhouse gases. Burning fossil fuels produces carbon dioxide, which plays a large part in climate change. Drilling also releases methane, a strong greenhouse gas, worsening global warming. Releasing gas affects the planet's ecosystems, causing more extreme weather and the loss of plant and animal life. Lastly, drilling can cause social and economic problems. Drilling operations can disturb local communities, forcing people to move and lose their traditional living methods. Moreover, extracting natural resources can also lead to political problems and conflicts. Disputes often arise in places where oil and gas money are shared unfairly.

Oil and gas drilling is an essential energy source with many environmental and health risks. Investing in clean energy sources like wind and solar power and using better practices for finding and extracting fossil fuels is essential to lower these risks and create a more sustainable future.

(280 words)

1 Vocabulary Check

Fill in the blanks with the most appropriate word from the list below.

1. The government initiated another (   ) to secure natural resources.
2. Some people were worried that the new facility might (   ) the local environment.
3. Scientists utilized an innovative technology to (   ) the deep ocean floor.
4. Environmental activists gathered in front of the factory because it had decided to (   ) substances which were potentially harmful.
5. The buzzer alerts the residents when a gas (   ) occurs.

release	harm	operation	leak	explore

2 Comprehension Questions

Answer the following questions in English.

1. When can spills and leaks happen?

2. What happens if harmful chemicals are released?

3. Why does fracking cause earthquakes?

4. Why is methane bad for the environment?

5. What happens when local people are forced to move as a result of drilling operations?

3 Grammar Check

Unscramble the following words and complete the sentences.

1. A couple of violations were found at [inspection, factory, during, annual, the, the].

   A couple of violations were found at [   ].

2. Tom experienced Japanese traditional [to, from, the, the, pottery, beginning, making, end].

   Tom experienced Japanese traditional [

   _____].

3. The government will increase funding for the energy industry, [decrease, been, pressure, has, under, which, to] CO_2 emissions.

   The government will increase funding for the energy industry, [

   _____] CO_2 emissions.

Ⅲ Discussion

インターネットなどを利用し，新エネルギー，代替燃料について調べましょう。
石油やガスの掘削によるリスクから環境や人々の健康を守りながら，必要なエネルギーを
確保するにはどうしたらいいのでしょうか。風力発電や太陽光発電などはこの問題の解
決にどのような役割を果たせるでしょうか。新エネルギー，代替燃料の問題点，その問
題の解決方法について検討し，主張，理由など自らの考えをまとめ，発表しましょう。

新エネルギーの種類とその問題点について 調べてみましょう。

New energy	Problems
(例) hydrogen 　　 biofuel	(例) explosion 　　 rising prices of crops

Discussion Topic

How can we make sure that we get the energy we need while also protecting the environment and people's health from the risks of oil and gas drilling?
What part should other energy sources, like wind and solar power, play in solving this problem, and what difficulties might they face in becoming more widely used?

Memo

Opinion

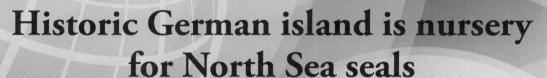

Lesson 16

Historic German island is nursery for North Sea seals

エコツーリズムと一般的な観光を組み合わせることで，環境，地域の人々，ビジネスに貢献し，観光客に休暇を楽しんでもらうためにはどうすれば良いでしょうか。

Ⅰ Listening

1 Key Word Study ◀ — Before Watching the Video —

Match each word with its definition.

1. adulthood   (   )   2. consequence (   )   3. delight   (   )

4. enthusiast   (   )   5. newborn   (   )   6. observer   (   )

7. photographer (   )   8. temperature (   )   9. weigh   (   )

10. windy   (   )

a．観察者	b．影響	c．温度	d．生まれたばかりの
e．風が強い	f．重さが～である	g．写真家	h．愛好家
i．喜び	j．成人期，成獣期		

2 Listening Practice 1 ◀ — First Viewing —

(Time 02:16) WEB動画 📺 DVD

Watch the news clip and write T if the statement is true or F if it is false.

1. Wildlife enthusiasts are watching seals on the beach of the Heligoland-Düne Island.
                                                                    (   )

2. A seal with a lot of white fur is about four years old.   (   )

3. The seal populations have become unmanageable since too many babies have been born.   (   )

4. More and more seals are coming to the island because there is lots of food. (   )

5. The baby seals will return to the island in spring.   (   )

109

Listening Practice 2

Listen to the recording and fill in the missing words.

Narrator: On this windy winter's day, this group of wildlife enthusiasts are seal watching on the beach of the Heligoland-Düne Island.

Elmar Ballstaedt: We're at the end of the birthing season,
5   how old do you think this baby seal is? Six weeks? Why?

Woman: Because he still has lots of white fur.

Elmar Ballstaedt: Yes, that's why. That one is around four weeks old.

10 **Narrator:** Around a thousand of the animals flock to this archipelago in the North Sea for the birthing season between November and January. But it's the newborn seal pups ¹( )

15   ( ) ( ) ( )
( ) ( ) ( )
( ).

Karen: They are so close, so alive. I often see them on television, but it's even more exciting here.

20 **Narrator:** For safety, tourists and photographers are asked to stay 30 meters away from the animals who can weigh up to 300 kilos when they reach adulthood and have been known to bite ²( ) ( )
( ) ( ). Keeping an eye on
25   both the seals and their observers are volunteers from the Jordsand Association and two rangers employed by Heligoland's Town Hall.

Ute Pausch: Sometimes, tourists forget their limits and get too close.
30   This has negative consequences in the summer because the seals

get used to people. They'll want to play in the water, and
³( ) ( ) ( )
( ).

Heligoland-Düne Island
ヘルゴラント島（ドイツ連邦
共和国領の北海の小さな島）
＊Heligoland（英語表記）
Helgoland（独語表記）

pup アザラシなどの子

35 **Narrator:** To keep excited tourists from getting too close, especially during birthing season, wooden boardwalks have been created. For now, the populations are manageable even if sometimes, a cheeky youngster makes its way ^{4}( ) ( )

40 ( ). But some fear a rise in water temperatures and levels could lead to greater seal numbers, leaving less space for both seals and enthusiastic tourists.

cheeky ずうずうしい

45 **Elmar Ballstaedt:** There are more and more of them, and I think it's because there's lots of food here. But we're at sea level here, and ^{5}( ) ( ) ( ) ( ) ( ), we'll probably have new challenges to face.

50 **Narrator:** The Jordsand Association says there have been more than 520 births since November. Once weaned, the baby seals will head to the water of the North Sea, but they will return in spring to change their fur, much to the delight of photographers and wildlife observers.

wean 離乳させる

4 Comprehension Check — Second Viewing —

WEB動画 DVD

Watch the news clip again and answer the following questions in English.

1. When is the birthing season of seals in the North Sea?

2. How far are tourists and photographers asked to stay away from the animals for safety?

3. Why do negative consequences happen in the summer?

4. What have been created to keep tourists from getting too close to the seals?

5. How many births have been reported since November according to the Jordsand association?

Listen to the recording and complete the summary.

During the birthing season between November and January, thousands of [1](   ) come to the beach of the Heligoland-Düne Island in the North Sea. Although the populations are currently [2](   ), some people are concerned that rising temperatures and sea levels could lead to an increase in the number of

5 seals and [3](   ) space issues for both seals and tourists. If water levels rise, new [4](   ) may need to be faced. Once the young seals are strong enough, they will head to the North Sea, but will return in spring to change their fur, providing an [5](   ) for photographers and wildlife enthusiasts.

II Reading 🎧(2-24)

Eco-tourism, also known as green tourism, focuses on protecting the environment while seeking to give travelers proper access to enjoy nature and outdoor

5 life. In recent years, this type of tourism has become popular because of the negative impacts that mass tourism has on landscape, wildlife, and local people.

The idea of eco-tourism promotes more awareness of nature and aims to reduce the

10 harmful effects of large-scale tourism.

Those who support this form of tourism ask businesses to preserve and sustain the environment by investing in projects that conserve nature. Steps include assisting NGOs and local groups to tackle issues that affect ecosystems. Eco-tourism can contribute to these efforts by providing a source of learning and income through eco-

15 friendly, sustainable activities. Supporters urge tourists to respect local cultures and customs by observing local people. In this way, tourists see where they should eat or buy and learn what actions to take in that culture. For example, asking tourists to use public transport or stay in eco-friendly housing can help sustain nature by lowering their carbon footprint. Other activities might be to reduce plastic use or not

20 buy fake goods. Eco-tourism also helps to boost the local economy by creating paid jobs. Giving local people chances to work helps reduce poverty and improves the overall quality of life for those living there. Local jobs also support the community

by keeping money within the local economy rather than channeling it to multinational businesses.

Eco-tourism shows it is possible to find a way to preserve the environment while bringing economic rewards. By carefully managing and promoting good tourist practices, investing in education, and supporting local people, it may be possible to protect nature and allow everyone to enjoy all it offers.

(288 words)

1 Vocabulary Check

Fill in the blanks with the most appropriate word from the list below.

1. You should be careful not to purchase (　　　　　) brand goods when shopping online.
2. Different countries have different policies regarding (　　　　　) smoking.
3. Clean air and oxygen are necessary in order to (　　　　　) life.
4. The hotel decided to (　　　　　) in a new water purifier.
5. Wearing a cold towel around your neck helps (　　　　　) body temperature.

invest	fake	public	lower	sustain

2 Comprehension Questions

Answer the following questions in English.

1. What does eco-tourism focus on?

_____

2. What can eco-tourism promote?

_____

3. What do supporters of eco-tourism urge tourists to do?

_____

4. How can eco-tourism help to boost the local economy?

_____

5. How can local jobs support the community?

_____

Unscramble the following words and complete the sentences.

1. Thomas [to, than, domestically, rather, decided, going, travel] abroad this summer.

   Thomas [   ] abroad this summer.

2. The passenger [the, slow, driver, asked, down, to, taxi] so that he could take pictures of the beautiful view.

   The passenger [   ] so that he could take pictures of the beautiful view.

3. Paris [one, the, as, of, world's, known, is] culinary capitals.

   Paris [   ] culinary capitals.

III Discussion

環境保護と経済発展を両立させる際の問題点について調べましょう。
エコツーリズムと一般的な観光を組み合わせることで，環境，地域の人々，ビジネスに
貢献し，観光客に休暇を楽しんでもらうためにはどうすれば良いでしょうか。
環境保護の問題点，経済発展の問題点，その両立，解決方法について検討し，主張，理
由など自らの考えをまとめ，発表しましょう。

エコツーリズムにおける環境保護と経済発展それぞれの 効果と問題点について調べてみましょう。

Environment	Economy	Problems
(例) preserve wild habitat	(例) local business	(例) over tourism

Discussion Topic

How can we combine eco-tourism ideas with regular tourism to help the environment,
local people, and businesses while also making sure tourists enjoy their vacations?

Memo

Opinion

115

Web動画のご案内　**StreamLine**

本テキストの映像は、オンラインでのストリーミング再生になります。下記URLよりご利用ください。なお**有効期限は、はじめてログインした時点から1年半**です。

http://st.seibido.co.jp

❶

ログイン画面

テキストに添付されているシールをはがして、12桁のアクセスコードをご入力ください。

同意してログイン

以下の「利用規約」をご確認頂き、同意する場合は上記ボタン【同意してログイン】を押してください。

利用規約

1. このウェブサイト（以下「本サイト」といいます）は、株式会社成美堂（以下「弊社」といいます）が運営しています。弊社の商品・サービス（以下「本サービス」といいます）利用時の会員登録の有無を問わず、本サイトの利用にあたっては、以下ご利用条件をお読み頂き、これらの条件にご同意の上ご利用ください。

2. 本サービスに関して個別に利用規約がある場合、本規約に加えそれらも適用されます。

3. 本サイトを通じて、弊社の商品を販売する第三者のウェブサイトにご案内ないしリンクされることがあります。リンク先ウェブサイトにおいて提供された個人情報は

> 巻末に添付されているシールをはがして、アクセスコードをご入力ください。

❷

メニュー画面

AFP World Focus
−Environment, Health, and Technology−
アクセスコード有効期限：2018年4月30日

🎬 **Video**　　🎵 **Audio**

Lesson 1: Global Warming and Climat... ❯
Lesson 2: Diet and Health for Long ... ❯
Lesson 3: Self-Driving for the Futu... ❯
Lesson 4: Sustaining Biodiversity a... ❯
Lesson 5: 3D Printers for Creating ... ❯
Lesson 6: IT and Education ❯
Lesson 7: Protection from Natural D... ❯
Lesson 8: Practical Uses of Drones ... ❯

> 「Video」または「Audio」を選択すると、それぞれストリーミング再生ができます。

❸

再生画面

AFP World Focus
−Environment, Health, and Technology−
アクセスコード有効期限：2018年4月30日

Lesson 2:
Diet and Health for Long Lives
食習慣：長生きのためのスーパーフードを探す

推奨動作環境

【**PC OS**】
Windows 7~　/　Mac 10.8~

【**Mobile OS**】
iOS 7~ / Android 4.x~

【**Desktop** ブラウザ】
Internet Explorer 9~ / Firefox / Chrome / Safari / Microsoft Edge

TEXT PRODUCTION STAFF

edited by 編集

Minako Hagiwara 萩原 美奈子

cover design by 表紙デザイン

Ruben Frosali ルーベン・フロサリ

CD PRODUCTION STAFF

narrated by 吹き込み者

Howard Colefield (AmE) ハワード・コールフィールド（アメリカ英語）

Karen Haedrich (AmE) カレン・ヘドリック（アメリカ英語）

Rachel Walzer (AmE) レイチェル・ワルザー（アメリカ英語）

Dominic Allen (AmE) ドミニク・アレン（アメリカ英語）

AFP World News Report 7
AFPニュースで見る世界7

2024年1月20日　初版発行
2024年2月15日　第2刷発行

著　　者　宍戸 真
　　　　　Kevin Murphy
　　　　　高橋 真理子

発 行 者　佐野 英一郎

発 行 所　株式会社 成 美 堂
　　　　　〒101-0052　東京都千代田区神田小川町3-22
　　　　　TEL 03-3291-2261　FAX 03-3293-5490
　　　　　https://www.seibido.co.jp

印 刷・製 本　三美印刷株式会社

ISBN 978-4-7919-7288-3　　　　　　　　　Printed in Japan